P9-EDQ-980

Microsoft® PowerPoint® 2010:
LEVEL 2 of 3

ALEC FEHL
Asheville-Buncombe Technical Community College

LABYRINTH
LEARNING™

El Sobrante, CA

Microsoft PowerPoint 2010: Level 2
by Alec Fehl

Copyright © 2011 by Labyrinth Learning

LABYRINTH
LEARNING™

Labyrinth Learning
P.O. Box 20818
El Sobrante, California 24820
800.522.9746
On the web at lablearning.com

President:
Brian Favro

Product Development Manager:
Jason Favro

Managing Editor:
Laura A. Lionello

Production Manager:
Rad Proctor

eLearning Production Manager:
Arl S. Nadel

Editorial/Production Team:
John Barlow, Teresa Bolinger, Belinda
Breyer, Sandy Jones, PMG Media,
Sheryl Trittin

Indexing: Joanne Sprott

Interior Design:
Mark Ong, Side-by-Side Studios

Cover Design:
Words At Work

All rights reserved. Printed in the United States of
America. No part of this material protected by this
copyright notice may be reproduced or utilized in
any form or by any means, electronic or
mechanical, including photocopying, recording,
scanning, or by information storage and retrieval
systems without written permission from the
copyright owner.

No part of this publication may be reproduced or
transmitted in any form or by any means without
the prior written permission from the publisher.

Labyrinth Learning™ and the Labyrinth Learning
logo are registered trademarks of Labyrinth
Learning. Microsoft®, Outlook®, PowerPoint®,
and Windows® are registered trademarks of
Microsoft Corporation. Other product and
company names mentioned herein may be the
trademarks of their respective owners.

The example companies, organizations, products,
people, and events depicted herein are fictitious.

No association with any real company,
organization, product, person, or event is intended
or should be inferred.

Screen shots reprinted with permission from
Microsoft Corporation.

ITEM: 1-59136-321-7
ISBN-13: 978-1-59136-321-7

Manufactured in the United States of America.

10 9 8 7 6 5 4 3 2 1

Table of Contents

Quick Reference Tables

Preface

Microsoft® PowerPoint® 2010: Level 2 provides thorough training of PowerPoint 2010 intermediate skills. This course is supported with comprehensive instructor resources and our eLab assessment and learning management tool. And, our new work-readiness exercises ensure students have the critical thinking skills necessary to succeed in today's world. After completing this course, students will be able to successfully face the challenges presented in the next book in this series, *Microsoft PowerPoint 2010: Level 3*.

Visual Conventions

This book uses many visual and typographic cues to guide students through the lessons. This page provides examples and describes the function of each cue.

Type this text	Anything you should type at the keyboard is printed in this typeface.
	Tips, Notes, and Warnings are used throughout the text to draw attention to certain topics.
Command→ Command→ Command, etc.	This convention indicates how to give a command from the Ribbon. The commands are written: Ribbon Tab→Command Group→Command→ Subcommand.
FROM THE KEYBOARD Ctrl+S to save	These margin notes indicate shortcut keys for executing a task described in the text.

Exercise Progression

The exercises in this book build in complexity as students work through a lesson toward mastery of the skills taught.

- **Develop Your Skills** exercises are introduced immediately after concept discussions. They provide detailed, step-by-step tutorials.
- **Reinforce Your Skills** exercises provide additional hands-on practice with moderate assistance.
- **Apply Your Skills** exercises test students' skills by describing the correct results without providing specific instructions on how to achieve them.
- **Critical Thinking and Work-Readiness Skills** exercises are the most challenging. They provide generic instructions, allowing students to use their skills and creativity to achieve the results they envision.

A Note About Lesson and Page Numbering

You will notice that this book does not begin with Lesson 1 on page 1. This is not an error! The lessons in this book are part of a larger text. We have repackaged the large book into smaller books – while retaining the original lesson and page numbering – to accommodate classes of varying lengths and course hours.

All content in this book is presented in the proper, intended order.

Preparing a Presentation

LEARNING OBJECTIVES

After studying this lesson, you will be able to:

- Edit document properties
- Create and print speaker notes
- Use proofing tools such as Spell Check, Find, and Replace
- Configure and print handouts
- Create slide headers and footers
- Create agenda and hyperlinked summary slides
- Draw on slides during a slide show

PowerPoint 2010 supplies you with robust tools for both the development and delivery of your presentation. Throughout this lesson, you will focus on the automatic editing features of PowerPoint 2010 as well as the slide show delivery options. All of these tools work together to refine and polish the presentation so that it is visually pleasing, grammatically correct, and effortlessly delivered.

Preparing the Presentation

Green Clean is a janitorial product supplier and cleaning service contractor to small businesses, shopping plazas, and office buildings. Tommy Choi (Green Clean's president) and Jenna Mann (his administrative assistant) have worked hard to create several presentations to promote the business. With the style, graphics, and animation in place, Jenna uses PowerPoint's editing tools to check that the spelling is correct. Tommy uses the enhanced Slide Show toolbar and begins to work on the delivery of the presentation. Knowing that people need to be a part of the presentation to remember it, Tommy is especially interested in making his presentation interactive. He asks Jenna how he can incorporate a dynamic approach to his presentation. Jenna recommends that they add a summary slide to give the presentation an agenda. Jenna also demonstrates the uses of the Pointer tool that Tommy can use during the presentation to emphasize points. They both decide that creating handouts will help the audience remember the services of Green Clean. They go back to work on the presentation with renewed enthusiasm.

green clean

*Our Services
*Products Sold
*Monthly Events
*Administrative Staff
*Welcome Aboard Specials
*Our Recent Success
*Contact Us
*More Information

*Summary

Green Clean Janitorial Service   10   10/24/2010

5.1 Preparing a Presentation

Video Lesson   labyrinthelab.com/videos

PowerPoint 2010 has printing and editing features that can help you prepare for a presentation and give attendees a printed copy of it.

- **Speaker notes:** You can draft and print notes about what you will say as each slide is displayed.
- **Editing tools:** You can use Spell Check, Find and Replace, and smart tag features to polish the presentation.
- **Printed handouts:** You can select from a variety of formats to print the presentation on paper for distribution.

Creating Speaker Notes

It's a known fact: Speaking before a group can be intimidating. Even an experienced presenter feels a flurry of anxiety before a presentation. The best way to thwart that anxiety is to be fully prepared. Consider using speaker notes to help with your delivery. *Speaker notes* are printable comments that you add to slides. They are not visible to the audience. Speaker notes can help you stay on track because if you suddenly freeze, you will be able to scan the notes you carefully prepared to keep your delivery style smooth. Using speaker notes can help you deliver an enthusiastic, informative presentation with confidence.

*General office and storefront cleaning
*Restroom sanitation
*Recycling pickup
*Consulting

*Our Services

Green Clean Janitorial Service   3   10/24/2010

Mention the 2009 Green USA magazine article ranking us as the most eco-friendly janitorial service.

The Notes view lets you draft notes to be printed with a miniature view of each slide.

| QUICK REFERENCE | ADDING SPEAKER NOTES |

Task	Procedure
Add speaker notes to a specific slide	■ Select the slide in Normal or Slide Sorter view. ■ Choose View→Presentation Views→Notes Page from the Ribbon. ■ Type your note in the area below the slide.
View speaker notes	■ Choose View→Presentation Views→Normal or choose View→Presentation Views→Notes Page from the Ribbon. ■ Select the desired slide. ■ In Normal view, speaker notes are displayed below the slide in a small scrolling box. ■ In Notes Page view, speaker notes are displayed below the slide in a large box.
Print speaker notes	■ Choose File→Print. ■ From the Print Layout menu, select Notes Pages. ■ Click OK.

DEVELOP YOUR SKILLS 5.1.1

Add Speaker Notes

In this exercise, you will add speaker notes to a few slides of the Green Clean Notes presentation.

1. **Open** the Green Clean Notes presentation from the Lesson 05 folder.

2. Make sure that the PowerPoint window is **maximized** ▣ .
   This ensures that the buttons on the Ribbon will match the figures for this lesson.

3. Choose **View→Presentation Views→Notes Page** 🗐 from the Ribbon.
   PowerPoint displays a full-screen view that includes the current slide and the notes area. However, notice that the phrase Click to Add Text *in the notes area is difficult to read.*

4. Adjust the zoom control percentage on the **Zoom** slider in the bottom-right corner of the PowerPoint window to **100%**, as shown in the following illustration.

5. If necessary, **scroll** until the phrase *Click to Add Text* is visible in the notes section on the title slide.

6. **Click** on the phrase *Click to Add Text* and type the following replacement phrase:
   Don't forget to thank the following people:

7. **Tap** Enter to move the insertion point to the next line, and then **type** the following three lines, **tapping** Enter after each line except the last:

   Talos Bouras - Sales Manager Enter
   Michael Chowdery - Purchasing Manager Enter
   Ahn Tran - Office Manager

   You can apply formatting to the content of speaker notes by using the same techniques used on slides.

8. **Select** (highlight) the last three lines you just typed and choose **Home→Paragraph→Bullets** from the Ribbon.

   PowerPoint applies bullets to the three selected lines, making the note easier to read. Your notes section should resemble the following figure.

9. Scroll through the presentation until you reach the **Our Services** slide and add the following text in the notes section: `Mention the 2009 Green USA magazine article ranking us as the most eco-friendly janitorial service`.

10. Scroll to the **Products Sold** slide and add the following text to the notes section: `Once again, mention Green USA magazine article`.

11. Scroll to the **Administrative Staff** slide and add the following text to the notes section: `Over 30 employees` [Enter] `Growing rapidly`.

12. **Select** the two lines you just typed and choose **Home→Paragraph→Bullets** from the Ribbon.

    At this point, four slides in your presentation should contain speaker notes.

View the Notes

13. Choose **View→Presentation Views→Normal** to switch to Normal view.

14. Choose **File→Print**.

15. Follow these steps to choose and preview the Notes Pages:

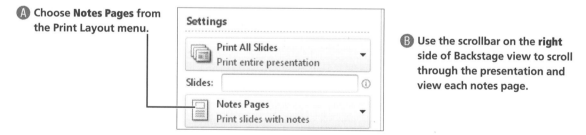

Ⓐ Choose **Notes Pages** from the Print Layout menu.

Ⓑ Use the scrollbar on the **right** side of Backstage view to scroll through the presentation and view each notes page.

16. Click the **Home** tab to close Backstage view without printing.

17. **Save** 💾 your presentation.

Editing Document Properties

Video Lesson   labyrinthelab.com/videos

Before making your presentations public, it is a good idea to identify the author, title, subject, and other details about the presentation. This information, called the Document Properties, is stored within the presentation file but is not visible on any slide or during a slide show. Specifying the Document Properties can be helpful when, several months after a presentation has been given, you need to determine who created the presentation or for what it was used. You can view and edit the Document Properties via the Document Panel.

The Document Panel can be turned on from the Info tab of Backstage view.

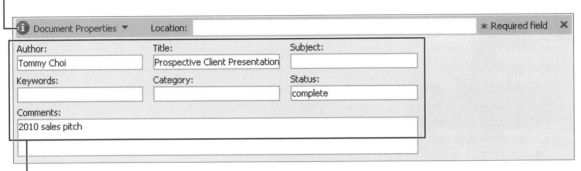

A variety of fields allow you to specify details about the presentation.

QUICK REFERENCE	DOCUMENT PROPERTY FIELDS
Field	**Possible Usage**
Author	Indicate the person or people who created the presentation.
Title	Show the title of the presentation.
Subject	Give the main idea of the presentation, similar to the subject line of an email.
Keywords	List words or short phrases that identify the main idea of the presentation, for example, "services offered, products sold, new client incentives."
Category	Indicate the broad category of the presentation, for example, "sales" or "prospective client presentation."
Status	Name the current status of the presentation, for example, "complete," "draft," or "obsolete."
Comments	Add notes, messages, or instructions you may wish to include for other people who may be working on the presentation or for people who are viewing the presentation on their own.

Edit Document Properties

In this exercise, you will edit the Document Properties of a presentation.

1. Click the **File** tab to display Backstage view.

2. Follow these steps to display the Document Panel:

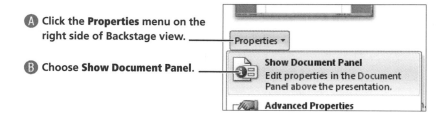

Ⓐ Click the **Properties** menu on the right side of Backstage view.

Ⓑ Choose **Show Document Panel**.

3. Follow these steps to edit the Document Properties:

Ⓐ Fill in the **Author, Title, Status,** and **Comments** fields as indicated.

Ⓑ **Close** the Document Panel.

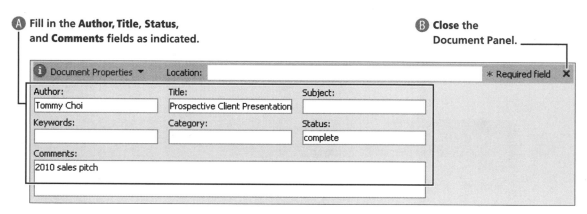

4. **Save** your presentation.

5.2 Editing Your Presentation

Video Lesson   labyrinthelab.com/videos

To assist you in editing your presentation, PowerPoint 2010 provides a powerful set of editing tools. The editing tools include Spell Check, Find, and Replace.

Using Spell Check Features

PowerPoint's Spell Check features work both automatically and manually to help you look for spelling errors in a presentation. By default, apparent spelling errors are flagged as you type, allowing you to easily identify possible errors and fix them manually. PowerPoint's AutoCorrect feature automatically corrects spelling errors as you type without flagging them. You can also perform a manual review of all content in a presentation.

Checking Spelling as You Type

If you are familiar with Microsoft Office, you probably have used the Spell Check command. PowerPoint's Spell Check feature automatically checks the entire presentation for misspelled words. To indicate a misspelled word, PowerPoint places a wavy red line under the word. You can right-click the misspelled word to display a shortcut menu with suggested replacements for the word. Choosing a replacement from this menu corrects the error as you work.

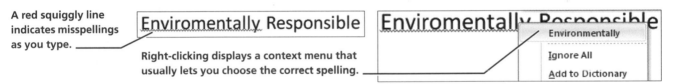

A red squiggly line indicates misspellings as you type.

Right-clicking displays a context menu that usually lets you choose the correct spelling.

The Spell Check Dictionary

PowerPoint installs with a dictionary of standard words. You can also add new words to PowerPoint's dictionary (which is also shared with the other Office Suite applications). For example, your industry may use special words not included in the standard dictionary. Adding such words to the dictionary prevents their being flagged as misspelled in the future. You can also tell the Spell Check feature to ignore a single instance of a word, or all instances of the word in this particular presentation, without actually adding it to the dictionary.

AutoCorrect

The AutoCorrect feature automatically corrects spelling errors as you type with no user intervention. PowerPoint keeps a list of common spelling errors mapped to the correct spelling. For example, *abbout* is mapped to *about*. Therefore, if *abbout* were typed on a slide, it would automatically be corrected and changed to *about*. AutoCorrect is also configured by default to correct words with two initial capitals, to capitalize the first letter of sentences, and to capitalize names of days.

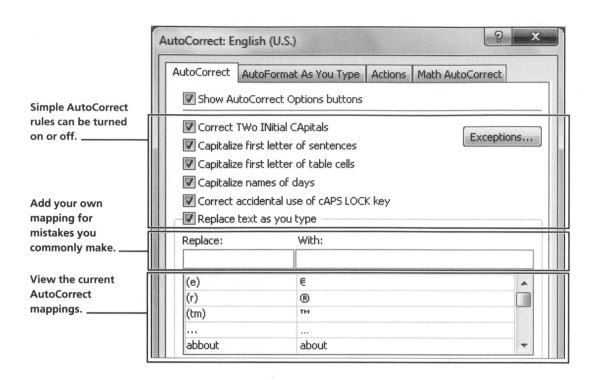

Simple AutoCorrect rules can be turned on or off. ⎯⎯⎯⎯⎯⎯⎯⎯

Add your own mapping for mistakes you commonly make. ⎯⎯⎯

View the current AutoCorrect mappings. ⎯⎯⎯⎯⎯⎯⎯

QUICK REFERENCE	WORKING WITH AUTOCORRECT
Task	**Procedure**
Access the AutoCorrect Options dialog box	■ Choose File→Options from the Ribbon. ■ Select the Proofing category. ■ Click the AutoCorrect Options button.
Create a custom mapping	■ Display the AutoCorrect Options dialog box. ■ Type the mistake you commonly make in the Replace text box, for example, *lodical*. ■ Type the correct spelling in the With text box, for example, *logical*. ■ Click the Add button.
Remove a custom mapping	■ Display the AutoCorrect Options dialog box. ■ Scroll through the list until you find the mapping you wish to remove. ■ Select the mapping and click the Delete button.

DEVELOP YOUR SKILLS 5.2.1

Use AutoCorrect

In this exercise, you will explore the features of AutoCorrect.

This exercise assumes that the spelling dictionary and AutoCorrect options have not been altered and are in their default state. If other students have used the computer before you to complete this exercise, it is likely the spelling dictionary and AutoCorrect options have already been configured. Check with your instructor to see whether your computer utilizes software such as Faronics Deep Freeze to reset any changes made to the system.

Use AutoCorrect

1. Choose the **title slide** of the presentation.

2. Choose **View→Presentation Views→Notes Page** from the Ribbon.

3. In the **Speaker Notes** section, click **after** the last line and **tap** Enter to create a new line.

4. Type the following (be sure to misspell *customer* as indicated):

   `Amy Wyatt - Cutsomer`

   The word customer *is misspelled, but AutoCorrect hasn't fixed it yet. You must indicate that you are through with a word by pressing* Enter *or* Spacebar*. You will do this in the next step.*

5. **Tap** Spacebar.
   The word is automatically corrected.

6. Continue typing **Service Rep** Enter so that the whole line reads *Amy Wyatt - Customer Service Rep* and an empty bullet appears in a new line.

Create a Custom Mapping

7. Type **Isaac Carter - intranet snd Website** (be sure to misspell *and* as *snd*).
   AutoCorrect did not correct the misspelling because replacing snd *with* and *is not a default mapping in PowerPoint. You can create custom mappings for words you mistype often.*

8. **Tap** the Backspace key several times until the words *snd Website* are deleted. The mouse pointer should be positioned just after the word *intranet*.

   - Amy Wyatt – Customer Service Rep
   - Isaac Carter - intranet

9. Choose **File→Options** from the Ribbon.

10. Select the **Proofing** category and then click the **AutoCorrect Options** button.

11. Follow these steps to create a custom mapping:

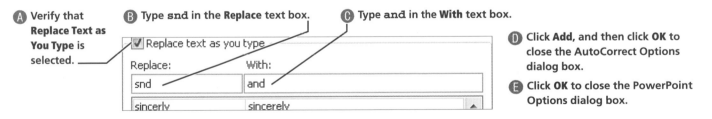

Ⓐ Verify that **Replace Text as You Type** is selected.

Ⓑ Type **snd** in the **Replace** text box.

Ⓒ Type **and** in the **With** text box.

Ⓓ Click **Add**, and then click **OK** to close the AutoCorrect Options dialog box.

Ⓔ Click **OK** to close the PowerPoint Options dialog box.

12. **Tap** the Spacebar and then type **snd Website**. Be sure to misspell *snd* again.
    The word is corrected automatically now that a custom mapping exists.

13. **Save** your presentation and continue with the next topic.

Using the Spelling Command

Video Lesson   labyrinthelab.com/videos

 You can also systematically review all spelling in the presentation with PowerPoint's Spelling command. This command reviews not only the slides but also the speaker notes for any incorrectly spelled words. The Spelling dialog box also offers additional choices not available in the shortcut spelling menu displayed when you right-click:

FROM THE KEYBOARD

F7 to run a spell check

- **Ignore/Ignore All:** Use the Ignore button to ignore the current instance of the word or use Ignore All to ignore every occurrence of the word throughout the presentation.
- **Change/Change All:** Use the Change button to change the current instance of the word to that chosen in the Change To box, or use Change All to change all occurrences of the word in the entire presentation.
- **Add:** Use the Add button to add the word to the dictionary.
- **AutoCorrect:** The AutoCorrect button uses the suggested word in the Change To box to automatically change the word on the slide. An AutoCorrect mapping is also added in the AutoCorrrect Options.
- **Close:** The Close button closes the Spelling dialog box.

The Options button jumps you directly to PowerPoint's Proofing options menu.

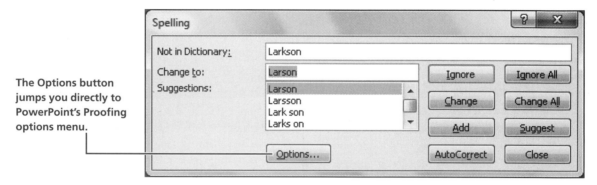

The Spelling dialog box offers more choices as compared to the right-click shortcut menu.

Spell Check is not infallible. Incorrect spellings of standard words won't always be caught—for example, "It's there problem now."

QUICK REFERENCE	INVOKING SPELL CHECK
Task	**Procedure**
Check spelling throughout the entire presentation	■ Choose Review→Proofing→Spelling ABC✓ from the Ribbon.
Check the spelling of a single word	■ Right-click the word you wish to check. ■ If the Spelling option appears in the pop-up context menu, select it to make the Spelling dialog box appear. ■ If the Spelling option does not appear in the context menu, the word exists in the dictionary and is probably spelled correctly.
Display and adjust PowerPoint's Proofing options	■ Choose File→Options. ■ Choose the Proofing category in the left panel.

Use Spell Check

In this exercise, you will explore the features of Spell Check.

This exercise assumes that the spelling dictionary and AutoCorrect options have not been altered and are in their default state. If other students have used the computer before you to complete this exercise, it is likely the spelling dictionary and AutoCorrect options have already been configured.

Use the Shortcut Menu

1. Choose **View→Presentation Views→Normal** from the Ribbon, and then select the **sixth slide**, Welcome Aboard Specials.

2. Click after the **last** sentence, **tap** ⌅Enter, and **type** the following, making sure to misspell as indicated:

   15% discount on EcoGreen brand cleening supplies

   EcoGreen is a brand name, so even though it is flagged as misspelled with a wavy red underline, we will ignore it for the moment. Cleening is misspelled and is flagged with a wavy red underline. It will have to be corrected.

3. **Right-click** *cleening* and choose *cleaning* from the shortcut menu.
   The spelling is corrected, and the wavy red underline disappears.

Use the Spelling Command

4. Choose **Review→Proofing→Spelling** 🔤 from the Ribbon.
   The Spelling dialog box appears, and the word EcoGreen *will most likely be displayed. Because this is a brand name, it is not a misspelling but rather an unrecognized spelling.*

5. Click **Ignore All** to ignore all instances of the word throughout all slides.
   The word is not added to the dictionary, so it will be flagged as a misspelling if it is used in other presentations. However, clicking Ignore All results in it no longer being flagged as misspelled in this presentation.

   Talos *was used in a speaker note on the title slide of the presentation. Although this name is spelled correctly, Spell Check reports it as an error because this name does not appear in the dictionary. Because this is a name you may use in other presentations, you will add it to the dictionary so it is never flagged as misspelled. Keep in mind that a different word may appear if you have spelling errors in your presentation that occur prior to the name* Talos.

6. Click the **Add** button to add the word *Talos* to the dictionary.
   At this point, Spell Check will continue to display words that it believes are misspelled.

7. Continue **spellchecking** the presentation, using your best judgment.

8. When the spell check is complete, **save** your presentation and continue with the next exercise.

Using the Custom Dictionary and AutoCorrect

Video Lesson   labyrinthelab.com/videos

Adding a word to the dictionary during a spell check permanently alters the dictionary that PowerPoint uses. This has an effect on future uses of PowerPoint because the added word will no longer be flagged as a misspelled word. On your home computer, that's fine. But in a school computer lab, it is nice to remove your custom words so other computer users can have the benefit of using PowerPoint in its default state.

QUICK REFERENCE	REMOVING CUSTOM WORDS FROM THE SPELLING DICTIONARY
Task	**Procedure**
Remove a custom word from the spelling dictionary	■ Choose File→Options from the Ribbon.
	■ Choose the Proofing category from the left side of the PowerPoint Options dialog box.
	■ Click the Custom Dictionaries button in the middle of the dialog box. The Custom Dictionaries dialog box opens.
	■ Click the Edit Word List button in the top-right corner of the Custom Dictionaries dialog box. The CUSTOM.DIC dialog box opens.
	■ Scroll through the word list and select the word you wish to remove.
	■ Click Delete to delete the selected word, or click Delete All to delete all the custom words.
	■ Click OK to close the CUSTOM.DIC dialog box.
	■ Click OK to close the Custom Dictionaries dialog box.
	■ Click OK to close the PowerPoint Options dialog box.

DEVELOP YOUR SKILLS 5.2.3
Clean Up the Custom Dictionary and AutoCorrect

In this exercise, you will remove all the custom words from the dictionary and remove custom AutoCorrect mappings so other computer users can use PowerPoint in its default state.

Reset the Custom Dictionary

1. Choose **File→Options** from the Ribbon.

2. Choose the **Proofing** category from the left side of the PowerPoint Options dialog box.

3. Click the **Custom Dictionaries** button in the middle of the dialog box.
   The Custom Dictionaries dialog box opens.

4. Click the **Edit Word List** button in the top-right corner of the Custom Dictionaries dialog box.
   The CUSTOM.DIC dialog box opens.

5. Click **Delete All** to delete all the custom words.

6. Click **OK** to confirm the deletion.

7. Click **OK** to close the CUSTOM.DIC dialog box.

8. Click **OK** to close the Custom Dictionaries dialog box.

Reset the AutoCorrect Custom Mappings

9. Click the **AutoCorrect Options** buttons at the top of the PowerPoint Options dialog box.

10. Type **snd** in the **Replace** box to quickly find the snd mapping you created earlier.
The AutoCorrect mapping snd *to* and *is highlighted.*

11. Click **Delete**, and then click **OK** to close the AutoCorrect dialog box.

12. Click **OK** to close the PowerPoint Options dialog box.

Using Find and Replace

Video Lesson   labyrinthelab.com/videos

As you edit the presentation, you may decide to replace one term with a new one. Use the Find feature to find a word or phrase in the presentation. What you do after you find it is up to you. You might make a correction, change the phrasing, or add or remove content from the slide. Using the Find and Replace feature, you can quickly search throughout the presentation for one term and replace it with another simultaneously. The Find and Replace dialog boxes are very similar. In fact, the Replace dialog is simply an extension of the Find dialog. Both allow you to type a word or phrase, or select from previously entered terms. The Find and Replace commands, like the Spelling command, search for text on both slides and speaker notes.

FROM THE KEYBOARD
CTRL+F for Find
CTRL+H for Replace

Three Useful Options

The Find and Replace dialog boxes have useful options to enhance searches:

- **Match Case:** You can make searches case sensitive, so that searching for *Dog* would not find *dog*.

- **Whole Word Only:** You can search for whole words only. For example, if you searched for *cat*, then *catalyst* and *scattered* would be found because they contain the characters c-a-t. With the Find Whole Words Only option enabled, a search for *cat* would find only *cat*.

- **Replace All:** The Replace All option, available from the Replace dialog box only, replaces all occurrences of the term with a single click throughout the entire presentation. This includes bulleted and non-bulleted text, slide titles, and speaker notes.

Note that the Find Whole Words Only option is not available if you enter more than one word in the Find What box.

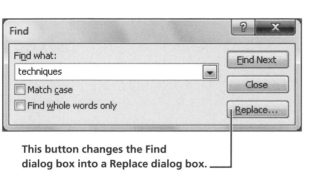
This button changes the Find dialog box into a Replace dialog box.

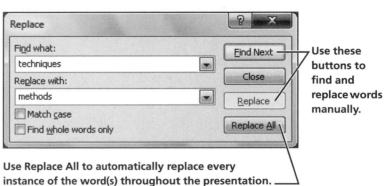
Use Replace All to automatically replace every instance of the word(s) throughout the presentation.

Task	Procedure
Find words	■ Choose Home→Editing→Find from the Ribbon, or use Ctrl+F from the keyboard. ■ Type the word you wish to find, set desired options, and then click Find Next.
Replace words	■ Choose Home→Editing→Replace from the Ribbon, or use Ctrl+H from the keyboard. ■ Type the word you wish to replace, set desired options, and then click Find Next. ■ Click Replace to replace a single instance of a word, or Replace All to replace all instances.

DEVELOP YOUR SKILLS 5.2.4
Use the Replace Command

In this exercise, you will replace text by using the Replace dialog box.

Replace Terms One at a Time

1. Select the **Our Services** slide and note that the second bullet says *Restroom*.

2. Select the **Products Sold** slide and note that the sixth bullet says *Restroom*.

3. Select the **Welcome Aboard Specials** slide and note the third bullet contains the word *Restroom*.
   You will change the word Restroom *to* Bathroom *on only two of the slides.*

4. Select the **first slide** in the presentation, the title slide.

5. Choose **Home→Editing→** 🔤 Replace from the Ribbon.

6. Type **Restroom** in the **Find What** box.

7. Type **Bathroom** in the **Replace** With box.

8. Remove any **checkmarks** from the Match Case or Find Whole Words Only Options.
   We want to find every instance of the word restroom, *regardless of whether it is capitalized.*

9. Click the **Find Next** button.
   The Our Services slide is displayed, and the word Restroom *is selected (highlighted).*

10. Click the **Replace** button to replace this instance of *Restroom* with *Bathroom*.
    The change is made, and the next occurrence is automatically found.

    The Products Sold slide is displayed, and the word Restroom *is selected (highlighted).*

11. Click the **Replace** button to replace this instance of *Restroom* with *Bathroom*.
    The change is made, and the third occurrence is automatically found.

    The Welcome Aboard Specials slide is displayed, and the word Restroom *is selected (highlighted).*

12. Click the **Close** button to close the Replace dialog box without replacing the word on the Welcome Aboard Specials slide.

13. Navigate to the **Our Services** and **Products Sold** slides and verify that *Restroom* has been replaced with *Bathroom*.

14. Navigate to the **Welcome Aboard Specials** slide and verify that *Restroom* was not replaced.

Replace All Terms in a Presentation

On second thought, you realize that Restroom *was a better word after all. You will use the Replace dialog to quickly revert all instances of* Bathroom *back to* Restroom.

15. Choose **Home→Editing→** ⟨🔤 Replace⟩ from the Ribbon.

16. In the **Find What** box, type **Bathroom**. In the **Replace With** box, type **Restroom**.

17. Select the **Match Case** checkbox to ensure that only occurrences of *Bathroom*, and not *bathroom*, are found.

18. Click the **Replace All** button.
    PowerPoint makes all the replacements throughout the presentation and displays a summary dialog box informing you that two replacements were made.

19. Click **OK** to close the informational dialog box.

20. Click **Close** to close the Replace dialog box.

21. Navigate to the **Our Services** and **Products Sold** slides and verify that the term *Bathroom* has been replaced with *Restroom*.

22. **Save** your presentation and continue with the next topic.

5.3 Printing Handouts

Video Lesson   labyrinthelab.com/videos

You can reinforce the main points of your presentation by providing your participants with handouts. Participants will be able to walk away from your presentation with more than a vague memory of your slide show; all of the facts you presented during the presentation will go with them as a reference. Handouts can be printed in a wide range of layouts, from two to nine slides per page. For example, printing three slides on a page places three small slides on the left side and multiple lines on the right for note taking.

Handout with three slides per page

Handout with six slides per page

Using Handout Masters

In any presentation, there is a single handout master that controls the format of the handout sheets. You can change the format of the handout master, which will affect all handouts in the presentation. This is helpful because you need only change a single handout master, and the layout, look, and feel of multiple handouts will be affected. Choosing View→Master Views→Handout Master from the Ribbon displays the Handout Master window and contextual tab. Options that you can set on the handout master, which affect all printed handouts, are summarized in the following table.

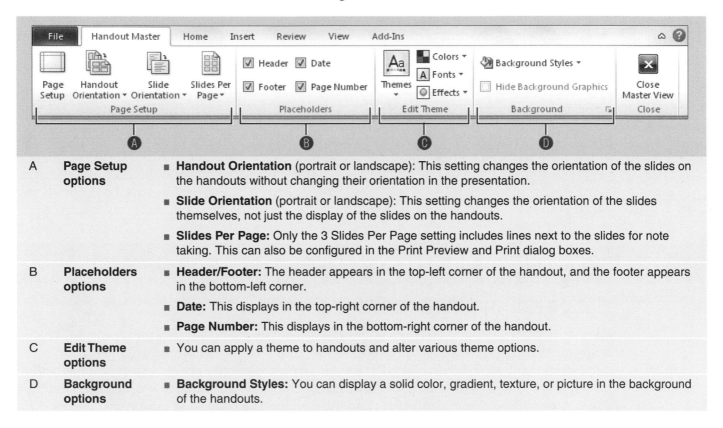

A	Page Setup options	■ **Handout Orientation** (portrait or landscape): This setting changes the orientation of the slides on the handouts without changing their orientation in the presentation.
		■ **Slide Orientation** (portrait or landscape): This setting changes the orientation of the slides themselves, not just the display of the slides on the handouts.
		■ **Slides Per Page:** Only the 3 Slides Per Page setting includes lines next to the slides for note taking. This can also be configured in the Print Preview and Print dialog boxes.
B	Placeholders options	■ **Header/Footer:** The header appears in the top-left corner of the handout, and the footer appears in the bottom-left corner.
		■ **Date:** This displays in the top-right corner of the handout.
		■ **Page Number:** This displays in the bottom-right corner of the handout.
C	Edit Theme options	■ You can apply a theme to handouts and alter various theme options.
D	Background options	■ **Background Styles:** You can display a solid color, gradient, texture, or picture in the background of the handouts.

Using Handout Headers and Footers

You can set up a header and footer to print on all pages of a handout. These work just like headers and footers in a word processor document. Headers appear at the top, or head, of the document. Footers appear at the bottom, or foot, of a document. Headers and footers often include the presenter's name, occasion, date, and other information, which is helpful when attendees reference the handouts later, after the presentation.

These headers will print at the top of each handout page.

Printing Handouts

Printing handouts is similar to printing slides. Printing handouts is a simple matter of changing printing options on the Print tab of Backstage view.

QUICK REFERENCE	WORKING WITH HANDOUTS
Task	**Procedure**
Design a handout master	■ Choose View→Master Views→Handout Master from the Ribbon. ■ Use the commands on the Master Handout tab to format your handouts. ■ Choose Handout Master→Close→Close Master View ✕ to return to your presentation.
Print handouts	■ Choose File→Print from the Ribbon. ■ From the Print Layout menu, select a handout layout.

DEVELOP YOUR SKILLS 5.3.1
Print Handouts with a Header and Footer

In this exercise, you will add the date and event to the header and footer of the handouts. The handouts will then be printed in a special layout.

Set Up a Handout Header and Footer

1. Choose **View→Master Views→Handout Master** from the Ribbon to display the handout master for the current presentation.

2. Follow these steps to set up header sheets:

Ⓐ Verify that all four of the **Placeholders** checkboxes are selected.

Ⓑ Scroll to the **top** of the handout, if necessary.

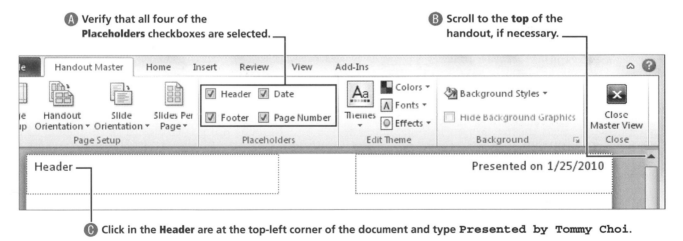

Ⓒ Click in the **Header** are at the top-left corner of the document and type `Presented by Tommy Choi`.

3. **Scroll down** to the bottom of the document, **click** in the bottom-left Footer placeholder, and type `Green Clean Janitorial Service`.

4. Choose **Handout Master→Close→Close Master View** ✕ from the Ribbon to close the handout master and return to the presentation.

Use Print Preview

5. Choose **File→Print**.

6. Follow these steps to set the handout layout:

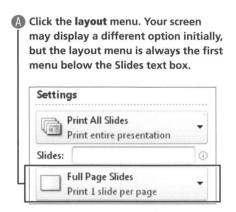

Ⓐ Click the **layout** menu. Your screen may display a different option initially, but the layout menu is always the first menu below the Slides text box.

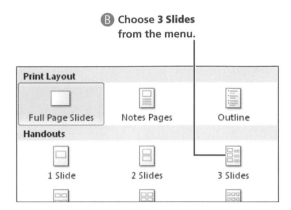

Ⓑ Choose **3 Slides** from the menu.

7. Use the **scroll bar** on the right side of Backstage view to browse through the pages.

8. Choose a different **handout format** from the layout menu, such as the six slides per page format.
   Notice that the three slides per page format is the only one that displays note lines.

9. Click the **Home** tab to exit Backstage view when you have finished.

10. **Save** your presentation and continue with the next exercise.

Using Slide Footers

Video Lesson	labyrinthelab.com/videos

Just as you can place a header or footer on a handout, you can also place footers on the slides in your presentation. Slide footers often display the date, event name, slide number, or other text that you want visible through the presentation. Although the term *footer* implies being inserted along the bottom of a slide, this will change depending on the slide layout and document theme. For example, some slide footers display along the top of the title slide. The same is true for the other elements, such as the slide number and date. These elements will display in different locations on a slide depending on the slide layout and document theme. Additionally, you may opt to display footers on all slides in the presentation, all slides except the title slide, or selected slides only.

Slide footers and handout footers are completely separate settings.

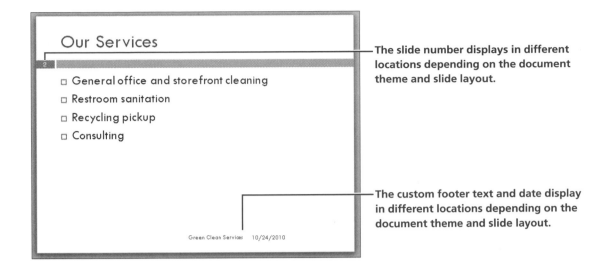

The slide number displays in different locations depending on the document theme and slide layout.

The custom footer text and date display in different locations depending on the document theme and slide layout.

Dating Slide Footers

If you choose to include the date, you will need to decide whether you want the date/time updated automatically so your presentation always displays the current date/time—or if you prefer to type in a static date/time that never changes unless you edit it manually. If you choose to update automatically, you have the option to display the date in several formats including numbers only, day or month spelled out, and even including the time.

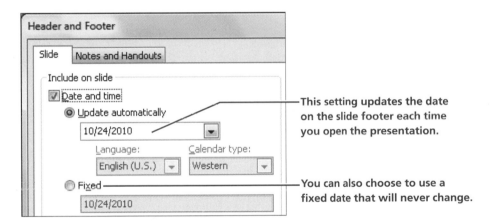

This setting updates the date on the slide footer each time you open the presentation.

You can also choose to use a fixed date that will never change.

QUICK REFERENCE	WORKING WITH SLIDE FOOTERS
Task	**Procedure**
Display the slide Header and Footer dialog box	▪ Select the slides(s) to which you want the command applied (not necessary if you will apply the settings to all slides in the presentation). ▪ Choose Insert→Text→Header & Footer 🖹 from the Ribbon. ▪ Make the desired settings, and then click Apply to All to add the header/footer to all slides in the presentation, or click Apply to add the header/footer to the selected slide(s).

Set Up a Slide Footer

In this exercise, you will create a slide footer and apply it to all slides in the presentation.

1. Choose the **Monthly Events** slide (the fourth slide in the presentation).

2. Choose **Insert→Text→Header & Footer** ⬚ from the Ribbon.

3. Follow these steps to configure your footer:

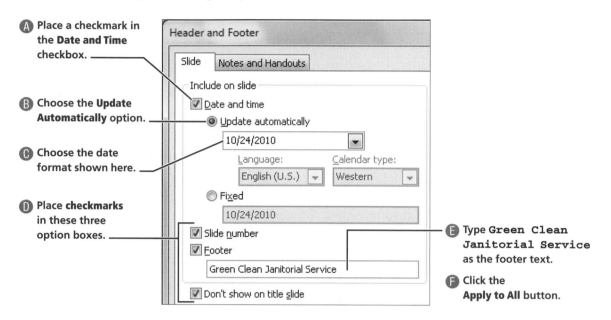

Ⓐ Place a checkmark in the **Date and Time** checkbox.

Ⓑ Choose the **Update Automatically** option.

Ⓒ Choose the date format shown here.

Ⓓ Place **checkmarks** in these three option boxes.

Ⓔ Type **Green Clean Janitorial Service** as the footer text.

Ⓕ Click the **Apply to All** button.

PowerPoint applies the settings to all slides in the presentation. You could have chosen to apply the footer to just the currently displayed slide. The footer should appear at the bottom of the Monthly Events slide, similar to the following figure.

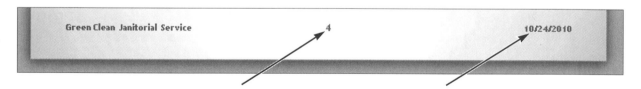

4. **Browse** through the presentation and notice that the slide number footer appears on every slide except the title slide.

5. **Save** your presentation and continue with the next topic.

Printing Transparencies

In addition to printing handouts and slides to share with your audience, you can also print transparencies to use with an overhead projector. While there is no Print Transparency option in PowerPoint, you can simply print your slides, handouts, or notes onto transparency film if your printer supports it. You will need to check the documentation for your printer to learn how to specify transparency film, as the steps vary from printer to printer.

5.4 Enhancing Presentation Navigation

Video Lesson   labyrinthelab.com/videos

Audience members can become anxious before a presentation if they have no idea how long the presentation will run or what topics will be covered. An agenda slide can help alleviate that anxiety. Additionally, if attendees have questions at the end of a presentation, a summary slide offers a visual recap of topics covered and can include navigation that aids the presenter in displaying previous slides without fumbling around trying to locate the desired slide.

Creating Agenda and Summary Slides

Many presentations begin with an agenda slide that outlines the various topics to be covered in the presentation and end with a summary slide that offers a brief recap of what was covered. Older versions of PowerPoint provided a Summary Slide tool that automated the process of creating a summary or agenda slide. This functionality was removed from PowerPoint 2007 and is still absent from PowerPoint 2010, so these slides must now be created manually. Savvy presentation designers often integrate hyperlinks in their summary slide, making the summary slide not only a review of the presentation, but a way to navigate to any slide quickly should attendees have questions about previous slides at the end of a presentation.

The overview offered by an agenda slide makes it easier for the audience to anticipate and follow the flow of your presentation.

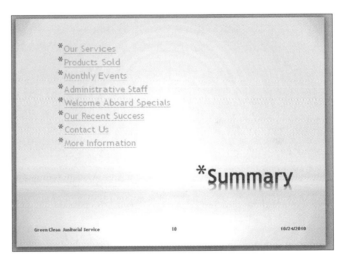

A summary slide offers the opportunity for the presenter to review what was covered in the presentation. Hyperlinks on the slide make it easy to jump back to specific parts of the presentation.

Create Agenda and Summary Slides

In this exercise, you will create an agenda slide and a summary slide.

Create an Agenda Slide

1. Select the **title slide** and choose **Home→Slides→New Slide** 🖼 from the Ribbon.

2. Type **Agenda** for the slide title, and then **type** the following in the text box:
   - **Our Services** `Enter`
   - **Products Sold** `Enter`
   - **Monthly Events** `Enter`
   - **Administrative Staff** `Enter`
   - **Welcome Aboard Specials** `Enter`
   - **Our Recent Success** `Enter`
   - **Contact Us**

   Notice that the bulleted text you just typed matches the titles of the slides in the presentation. The agenda slide is complete.

Create a Summary Slide

3. Select the **Agenda** slide from the Slides panel on the left side of the PowerPoint window, and then choose **Home→Clipboard→Copy** from the Ribbon.
   The entire slide is copied to the clipboard.

4. Select the **last slide**, Contact Us, and choose **Home→Clipboard→Paste** from the Ribbon.
   The Agenda slide is duplicated after the Contact Us slide, becoming the new last slide in the presentation.

5. Change the **title** of the last slide from *Agenda* to **Summary**.

6. **Save** your presentation and continue with the next topic.

5.5 Using Hyperlinks in Presentations

Video Lesson   labyrinthelab.com/videos

 If you've ever browsed a website, you have used hyperlinks. A *hyperlink* on a web page is text or an image that, when clicked, takes you to another web page. A hyperlink in PowerPoint functions the same as a hyperlink on a web page. You can create hyperlinks in PowerPoint that take you to another slide in the same presentation, open a file on your computer, or take you to a website (provided you are connected to the Internet).

Clicking the Products Sold hyperlink on the summary slide navigates the presenter to the Products Sold slide.

Inserting Hyperlinks

PowerPoint 2010 offers two ways to insert hyperlinks. Though there are slight differences between the two options, the method you choose depends largely on personal preference. This lesson focuses on the Hyperlink dialog box.

- **Hyperlink dialog box:** This method allows you to create hyperlinks that, when clicked, open an existing web page, an existing file, another slide in the current presentation, or an email program with the recipient's email address prefilled.

- **Action dialog box:** This method allows you to create hyperlinks or buttons that do everything a regular hyperlink will do, but can also launch other programs, play sounds, and accomplish other complex tasks. Additionally, actions can be made to work when clicked or when the presenter simply points to a hyperlink/button.

Creating Hyperlinks for Slide Navigation

Navigating a PowerPoint presentation does not have to be linear. In other words, you don't have to start with slide 1, go to slide 2, go to slide 3, and continue sequentially until the end. You already know that you can use the Slide Show toolbar to navigate to any slide, but using the toolbar can break the flow of your presentation because the pop-up menu may clash with the color scheme or document theme. An alternative is to create a slide of hyperlinks that navigate to each slide in the presentation. Hyperlinks can be created in Normal or Outline view, but when clicked, function only in Slide Show view.

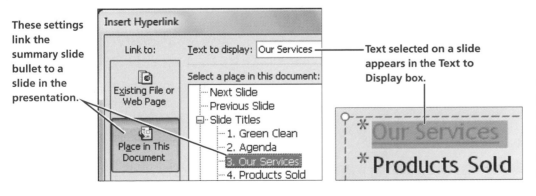

These settings link the summary slide bullet to a slide in the presentation.

Text selected on a slide appears in the Text to Display box.

You can integrate hyperlinks into a summary slide to allow quick navigation to any previous slide should attendees have questions or want to revisit a specific slide after the presentation.

QUICK REFERENCE	WORKING WITH HYPERLINKS
Task	**Procedure**
Insert a hyperlink	■ Select the text or object you wish to turn into a hyperlink. ■ Choose Insert→Links→Hyperlink 🌐 from the Ribbon. ■ In the Link To section on the left side of the dialog box, select the type of hyperlink (link to a file or web page, link to another slide in the presentation, or link to an email address). ■ Select the file, type the web page URL, select the slide, or type the email address. Then click OK.
Edit a hyperlink	■ Select the text or object that contains the hyperlink. ■ Choose Insert→Links→Hyperlink 🌐 from the Ribbon. ■ Modify your selection in the Edit Hyperlink dialog box and click OK.
Remove a hyperlink	■ Select the text or object that contains the hyperlink. ■ Choose Insert→Links→Hyperlink 🌐 from the Ribbon. ■ Click the Remove Link button at the bottom-right area of the Edit Hyperlink dialog box.

DEVELOP YOUR SKILLS 5.5.1

Add Hyperlinks to a Presentation

In this exercise, you will create hyperlinks on the existing Summary slide.

Create a Hyperlink to a Website

1. If necessary, select the **Summary** slide.

2. Click after the **last** line, Contact Us, and **tap** ⌨Enter⌨ to create a new blank line.

3. Type **More Information**.

4. **Select** the text you just typed and choose **Insert→Links→ Hyperlink** from the Ribbon to open the Insert Hyperlink dialog box.

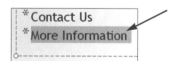

5. Follow these steps to create a link to a website:

Because Green Clean is a fictitious company, you will create the hyperlink to point to the Labyrinth Learning website.

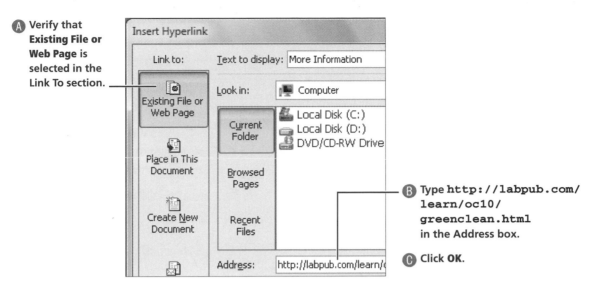

Ⓐ **Verify that Existing File or Web Page is selected in the Link To section.**

Ⓑ Type **http://labpub.com/ learn/oc10/ greenclean.html** in the Address box.

Ⓒ Click **OK**.

The More Information *text becomes underlined to indicate it is a hyperlink. It has also changed color to match the hyperlink color defined by the document theme.*

Create Hyperlinks to Two Slides

6. **Select** the text *Our Services* on the Summary slide so it becomes highlighted.

7. Choose **Insert→Links→Hyperlink** from the Ribbon to open the Insert Hyperlink dialog box.

8. Follow these steps to create a hyperlink to the Our Services slide:

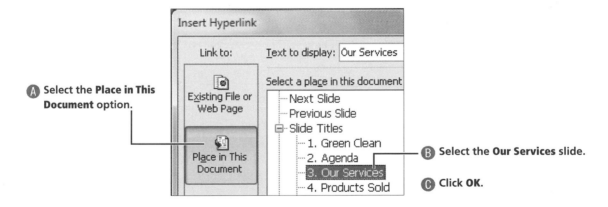

Ⓐ Select the **Place in This Document** option.

Ⓑ Select the **Our Services** slide.

Ⓒ Click **OK**.

The Our Services *text becomes underlined to indicate it is a hyperlink. It has also changed color to match the hyperlink color defined by the document theme.*

9. Select the **Products Sold** text, and then choose **Insert→Links→Hyperlink** from the Ribbon.
   Notice that Place in This Document *is already selected from the left side of the dialog box as PowerPoint has remembered your previous selection.*

10. Select the **Products Sold** slide and click **OK**.
    The Products Sold *text becomes underlined to indicate it is a hyperlink. It has also changed color to match the hyperlink color defined by the document theme.*

Finish the Navigation Slide

Now you will finish creating a navigation scheme from the Summary slide.

11. Follow these steps to add a hyperlink to the Monthly Events slide:
    ■ Select **Monthly Events** on the Summary slide.
    ■ Choose **Insert→Links→Hyperlink** from the Ribbon.
    ■ Choose the **Monthly Events** slide from the Slide Titles list, and then click **OK**.

12. Repeat **step 11** for the remaining four bulleted items on the Summary slide, creating links to the appropriate slides.
    You will test the hyperlinks in the next exercise.

13. **Save** 🖫 your presentation and continue with the next topic.

Repairing and Removing Hyperlinks

Video Lesson   labyrinthelab.com/videos

You can edit and remove hyperlinks in the Normal view by using the Hyperlink command. In most cases, the easiest way to open a hyperlink for editing is to choose a command from the shortcut menu after a right-click.

A right-click on a hyperlink displays useful editing commands.

The Necessity to Check Links

It is imperative that you check each and every hyperlink in a presentation. Your professional credibility is at risk if you lead a malfunctioning presentation. If you find during rehearsal that a hyperlink doesn't work, or that it isn't needed at all, you can easily repair or remove it.

Test and Repair Hyperlinks

In this exercise, you will test and repair hyperlinks.

Use Hyperlinks

1. Choose **Slide Show→Start Slide Show→From Beginning** 🖵 from the Ribbon.

2. **Click** through the presentation until you reach the Summary slide.

3. Click the **Our Services** hyperlink to immediately navigate to the Our Services slide.

4. Point to the **lower-left corner** of the slide to display the Slide Show toolbar.

5. Follow these steps to return to the Summary slide:

Notice that the Our Services hyperlink is now a different color. This indicates a visited link (a hyperlink that has been used).

6. Continue to test each of the other hyperlinks and verify that they navigate to the correct slide (remember, the More Information link will open your web browser and attempt to connect to the Labyrinth website). Use the **Slide Show toolbar** to return to the Summary slide when needed.

   If one of your hyperlinks navigated to the wrong slide, you will have the opportunity to fix it in the next few steps. If all of your hyperlinks worked, read through the next few steps to learn how to repair and remove hyperlinks should you have the need in the future.

7. **Tap** [Esc] to end the slide show and return to Normal view.

Repair Hyperlinks

8. **Click** once in the text of your bad hyperlink. If all of your links worked, click inside the **Our Services** text.
Note that the entire line does not have to be highlighted. Your cursor simply needs to be flashing in the text.

9. Choose **Insert→Links→Hyperlink** from the Ribbon.

10. Follow these steps to repair or remove a hyperlink:

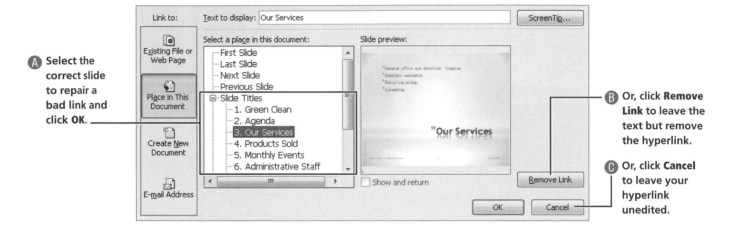

(A) Select the correct slide to repair a bad link and click **OK**.

(B) Or, click **Remove Link** to leave the text but remove the hyperlink.

(C) Or, click **Cancel** to leave your hyperlink unedited.

11. Continue to repair any hyperlinks necessary, and then view the slide show to test your repairs.

12. **Save** your presentation and continue with the next topic.

5.6 Using the Slide Show Toolbar

Video Lesson   labyrinthelab.com/videos

The Slide Show toolbar is enhanced in PowerPoint 2010. Normally when you begin a slide show, your mouse pointer is in the form of the Arrow tool, which is used to click slides or other objects on the slide. The Pointer option is used to select other tools, such as various pens and a highlighter, which enable you to draw, write, and highlight elements of your slides as you deliver the presentation.

Annotating with Pen Tools

FROM THE KEYBOARD

CTRL+P to change the pointer to Felt Tip Pen

CTRL+A to change the pointer to Arrow

As you deliver your presentation, the audience may ask for more detail on a key issue. With the Pointer options, you can immediately respond to the request by using the Pen or Highlighter to annotate slides, thus emphasizing important information. When the presentation ends, you will be asked whether you want to keep or discard any annotations. If you choose to keep them, they are saved with the presentation and will be there when you open it again and run the slide show. If you choose to discard the annotations, they disappear immediately and are not saved with the presentation. Examine the features of each Pointer tool in the table following the figure on the next page.

*25% discount for the first 30 days of and annual general cleaning contract

Wow!

*30% discount on all cleaning supply orders over $100

*One free Restroom Restoration package

*Offer expires July 20

*15% discount on EcoGreen brand cleaning supplies

*Welcome Aboard Specials

QUICK REFERENCE	USING PRESENTATION POINTER TOOLS
Tool	**Usage**
Choose a pointer tool	■ In Presentation mode, move the mouse pointer to make the Slide Show toolbar visible in the lower-left corner of the screen. ■ Click the Pointer options icon, and then choose the desired tool or ink color (see the following summary).
Summary of pointer tools	■ **Pen:** Draws and writes with different colors. ■ **Highlighter:** Highlights the text or image with a wide stroke of color. ■ **Eraser:** Removes all lines or highlighting from the slides. ■ **Ink Color:** You can choose from the full spectrum of colors available in PowerPoint to change ink color.

Use Pointer Options in a Slide Show

In this exercise, you will use each Pointer tool available in the Pointer menu.

Use the Pen Pointer Tool

1. In **Normal** view, select the title slide, and then choose **Slide Show→Start Slide Show→From Beginning** to begin the slide show presentation.

2. Follow these steps to navigate with the Slide Show toolbar:

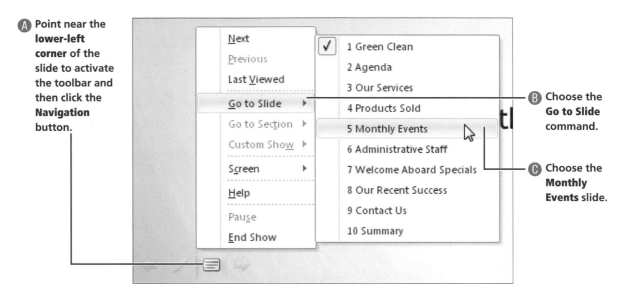

Ⓐ Point near the **lower-left corner** of the slide to activate the toolbar and then click the **Navigation** button.

Ⓑ Choose the **Go to Slide** command.

Ⓒ Choose the **Monthly Events** slide.

PowerPoint jumps you to the desired slide.

3. Click the **Pointer** on the toolbar, and then choose the **Pen**.
   The arrow turns into the point of a pen. You may need to move your mouse around a bit to see where the pointer is because the pen tip is very small.

4. Click the **Pointer** on the toolbar again, and then choose **Ink Color** and a shade of **red**.
   Notice the wide range of colors available to you.

5. Drag with the **Pen** tool to draw an oval around the *Family picnic Sunday* bullet as shown here:

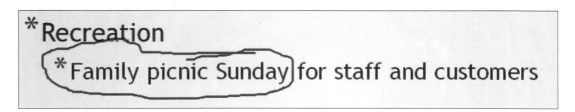

You might draw like this to emphasize this point during the presentation.

Use the Highlighter Tool

6. Click the **Navigation** 📃 button, point to **Go to Slide**, and click **Welcome Aboard Specials**.

7. Click the **Pointer** 🖊 button and choose the **Highlighter**.

8. **Drag** to highlight the *Offer expires* line as shown here:
   The Highlighter is really a wide stroke of color. You may wish to move it back and forth more than once to cover the text completely. The Highlighter tool is another useful way to emphasize a point during a presentation.

```
*One free Restroom Restora
*Offer expires July 20
*15% discount on EcoGreen
```

Change the Color of the Highlighter Tool

9. Choose **Slide Show Toolbar→Navigation** 📃 **→Go to Slide** and choose the **Contact Us** slide.

10. Choose the **Slide Show Toolbar→Pointer** button 🖊 **→Highlighter**.

11. Choose the **Slide Show Toolbar→Pointer** 🖊 button and choose the **Ink Color** tool. Choose any shade **other than** yellow.

12. **Highlight** the phone number as shown in the following illustration. Remember, you may have to drag the mouse across the text several times to achieve the desired thickness of the highlight.

```
Call
(800) 555-1212
or
```

Erase the Pointer Tool Annotations

13. Click the **Pointer** 🖊 tool and choose **Eraser**. Click once on the highlight to erase the highlighting on the slide.
    Notice that the highlighting is erased with one click of the mouse. The highlighting virtually disappears from the slide.

14. Click the **Pointer** 🖊 tool and choose **Arrow**.
    The Arrow tool lets you navigate the next slide by clicking.

15. Click to the **end** of the slide show. Choose **Discard** when prompted to save or discard the annotations.

16. **Save** 💾 your presentation and **exit** PowerPoint.

5.7 Concepts Review

Concepts Review   labyrinthelab.com/pp10

To check your knowledge of the key concepts introduced in this lesson, complete the Concepts Review quiz by going to the URL listed above. If your classroom is using Labyrinth eLab, you may complete the Concepts Review quiz from within your eLab course.

Reinforce Your Skills

Work with Speaker Notes

In this exercise, you will add speaker notes by using the Notes Page view.

1. **Start** PowerPoint and **maximize** the program window.

2. **Open** the sb-Tropical Getaways presentation from the Lesson 05 folder.

3. Choose **View→Presentation Views→Notes Page** from the Ribbon.

4. **Type** the following in the Notes text box below the first slide:

   `Welcome the employees to their new travel service` `Enter`

   `Thank Glenda Johnson - Director of Human Resources`

5. Use the **scroll bar** on the right side of the screen to navigate to the **Most Popular Destinations** slide and add the following to the speaker notes area:

   `Employees get a 35% discount on all destinations on the Popular Destinations list`

6. Use the **scroll bar** on the right side of the screen to navigate to the **Travel Now and Save!** slide and add the following to the speaker notes area:

   `12 preferred discount packages available to employees` `Enter`

   `No time limit on preferred discount packages` `Enter`

   `Limit of two packages per employee per year`

7. **Select** the text you just typed and choose **Home→Paragraph→Bullets** from the Ribbon to turn the three lines into a bulleted list.

8. **Save** 💾 your presentation and continue with the next exercise.

Use Spelling Check and Replace

In this exercise, you will check the spelling of a presentation and use the Replace command to replace words.

Before You Begin: The sb-Tropical Getaways presentation should be open.

Check Spelling

1. Choose **View→Presentation Views→Normal** from the Ribbon, and then select the **first slide**.

2. Choose **Review→Proofing→Spelling** to begin spellchecking the presentation.

3. Use the **Change** button in the Spelling dialog box to change *Liesure* to *Leisure*.

4. Use the **Change** button in the Spelling dialog box to change *Pakages* to *Packages*.

5. Use the **Change** button in the Spelling dialog box to change *Persin* to *Person*.

6. Click **OK** to close the message that the spell check is complete.

Use Replace

7. Choose **Home→Editing→Replace** to open the Replace dialog box.

8. In the **Find What** box, type `Categories` and in the **Replace With** box, type `Divisions`.

9. Select the **Match Case** checkbox so only *Categories* will be found and not *categories*.

10. Click **Find Next** to find the first occurrence of *Categories*.
    Categories *is found at the top of the Travel Categories page.*

11. Click **Replace** to replace the word.

12. Click **OK** to close the message window indicating that the search term cannot be found.

13. Click **Close** to close the Replace dialog box.

14. **Save** 🖫 your presentation and continue with the next exercise.

REINFORCE YOUR SKILLS 5.3

Print Handouts with a Header and Footer

In this exercise, you will add a header and footer to slide handouts and print handouts.

Before You Begin: The sb-Tropical Getaways presentation should be open.

Add Header/Footer

1. Choose **View→Master Views→Handout Master** from the Ribbon.

2. Select all four checkboxes in the **Placeholders** group.

3. In the **top-left corner** of the handout, in the Header section, type `Tropical Getaways`.

4. In the **bottom-left corner** of the handout, in the Footer section, type `New Employee Orientation`.

5. Choose **Handout Master→Close→Close Master View** from the Ribbon.

Print Handouts

6. Choose **File→Print** from the Ribbon.

7. Set the Print Layout option to **Handouts→3 Slides**.

8. Click the large **Print** button at the top of Backstage view.

9. **Save** 🖫 your presentation and continue with the next exercise.

Add Slide Footers

In this exercise, you will add footers to your slides.

Before You Begin: The sb-Tropical Getaways presentation should be open.

1. Choose **Insert→Text→Header & Footer** from the Ribbon.

2. Follow these steps to configure the slide footers:

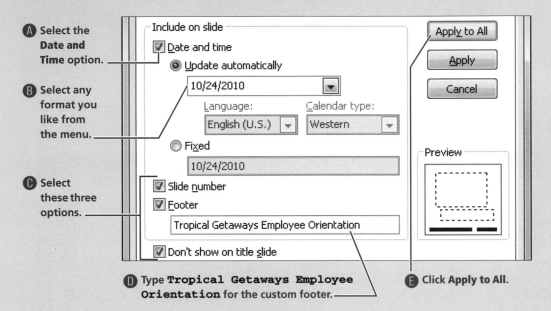

Ⓐ Select the **Date and Time** option.

Ⓑ Select any format you like from the menu.

Ⓒ Select these three options.

Ⓓ Type **Tropical Getaways Employee Orientation** for the custom footer.

Ⓔ Click **Apply to All**.

All slides except the title slide display the custom footer in the bottom-left corner, the date in the bottom-right corner, and the slide number in the circle just under the slide title.

3. **Save** 💾 your presentation and continue with the next exercise.

Add a Summary Slide with Hyperlinks

In this exercise, you will add a summary slide to the Tropical Getaways presentation.

Before You Begin: The sb-Tropical Getaways presentation should be open.

1. Select the **last slide**, Contact Us.

2. Choose **Home→Slides→New Slide** from the Ribbon.

3. Give the new slide a title of **Summary** and **type** the following in the text box:

   - **Opening** Enter
   - **Travel Divisions** Enter
   - **Most Popular Destinations** Enter
   - **Complete Packages** Enter
   - **Travel Now and Save!** Enter
   - **Contact Us**

4. **Double-click** the word *Opening* to select it, and then choose **Insert→Links→Hyperlink** from the Ribbon.

5. Follow these steps to link the word *Openings* to the title slide:

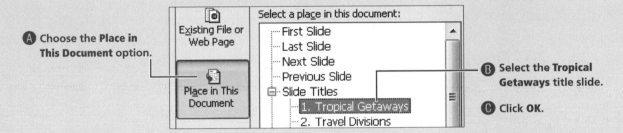

6. Repeat **steps 4** and **5** to link the rest of the bulleted text items to their corresponding slides.

7. Choose **Slide Show→Start Slide Show→From Beginning** from the Ribbon and navigate to the last slide, Summary.

8. **Click** a hyperlink to test it.

9. Return to the **Summary** slide and continue testing the other hyperlinks.

10. **Tap** Esc to end the slide show and return to Normal view.

11. If necessary, fix any hyperlinks that didn't work.

12. **Save** 💾 your presentation and continue with the next exercise.

Use Pointer Tool Options

In this exercise, you will draw on a slide during a presentation and test your hyperlinks.

Before You Begin: The sb-Tropical Getaways presentation should be open.

1. Choose **Slide Show→Start Slide Show→From Beginning** from the Ribbon.

2. Navigate to the **fourth slide**, Complete Packages.

3. Point to the **bottom-left corner** of the slide to display the Slide Show toolbar.

4. Click the **Pointer** options icon and select the Pen tool.

5. Draw a **line** around *Lodging 5 Days from $799.*

o Airfare	o 3 days from $599
o Lodging	o 5 days from $799
o Rental car	o 7 days from $999

6. **Tap** the [Spacebar] to navigate to the **sixth slide**, Contact Us.

7. Point to the **bottom-left corner** of the slide to display the Slide Show toolbar.

8. Click the **Pointer** options icon and select the Highlighter tool.

9. **Drag** several times across the phone number to highlight it.

10. Point to the **bottom-left corner** of the slide to display the Slide Show toolbar.

11. Click the **Pointer** options icon and select the Arrow tool.

12. Click anywhere on the slide to navigate to the **next slide**, Summary.

13. Click any of the **hyperlinks** to test them.

14. **Tap** [Esc] to end the slide show and return to Normal view.

15. Choose **Discard** when prompted to save your ink annotations.

16. **Save** 💾 and **close** your presentation.

Apply Your Skills

Add Speaker Notes and Use Spell Check

In this exercise, you will add speaker notes and use the Spell Check tool.

Add Speaker Notes

1. **Open** the as-Classic Cars presentation from the Lesson 05 folder.

2. Add the following **speaker notes** to the presentation:

   ■ Choose **Home→Paragraph→Bullets** to add bullets to your notes.

Slide	Speaker Notes
Classic Cars (title slide)	■ Thank the organizing committee ■ Welcome new members
Collections on Display	■ Thank collectors ■ Most valuable collection of classic cars in one location ■ 110 cars in mint condition
Door Prizes	■ No individual limits on winning ■ Mention the secret grand prize

Use Spell Check

3. Navigate to the **first slide** of the presentation and give the **Spelling** command.

4. Use your judgment to correct the spelling of the text.

5. Dismiss the Spell Check tool when you have finished checking the presentation and **save** the changes.

Use Replace and Pointer Options

In this exercise, you will work with the Replace feature and the Pointer tools.

Before You Begin: The as-Classic Cars presentation should be open.

Use Replace

1. Navigate to the **title slide**.

2. Use the following table to find and replace terms in the presentation:

Find	Replace With
techniques	methods
Vehicles	Automobiles
2004	2010

Use the Pointer Options

3. Run the slide show and navigate to the **second slide**, Collections on Display.

4. Using the **Pointer** options tool, highlight the phrase *Edsel highway*.

5. Next, choose the **third slide**, Workshops, and use the **Pen** to circle *Selling on the Internet*.

6. Have your instructor initial that this task was completed successfully. _____

7. Return to **Normal** view, discarding the ink annotations.

8. **Save** the presentation.

Work with Headers and Footers

In this exercise, you will add handouts with headers and footers to the presentation.

Before You Begin: The as-Classic Cars presentation should be open.

Add Headers and Footers to Handouts

1. Configure **headers and footers** for handouts as described in the following table:

Placeholder	Option to Choose or Type
Header	Classic Cars
Date	Enable the date and accept the default format
Footer	2010 Convention Highlights
Page Number	Enable the page number and accept the default format

2. Return to **Normal** view.

Add Slide Headers and Footers

3. Adjust the **slide header and footer** settings as follows:

Setting	Option to Choose or Type
Date and Time	Enable and set to Update Automatically. Choose any format you like.
Slide Number	Enable.
Footer	Enable and type `2010 Convention Highlights`.
Don't Show on Title Slide	Disable so the information displays on the title slide.

4. Apply the settings to all slides.

5. **Save** the presentation.

Create a Summary Slide with Hyperlinks

In this exercise, you will create a summary slide with hyperlinks.

Before You Begin: The as-Classic Cars presentation should be open.

1. Add a **new slide** to the end of the presentation, change the layout to **Title and Content**, and give it the title **Summary**.

2. **Type** the following for the slide's text:
   - ■ **Classic Cars**
   - ■ **Collections**
   - ■ **Workshops**
   - ■ **Prizes**

3. Create **hyperlinks** from the bulleted items to their corresponding slides. Classic Cars *should link to the title slide.*

4. **Run** the slide show and test the hyperlinks.

5. **Save** and **close** the presentation.

Critical Thinking & Work-Readiness Skills

In the course of working through the following Microsoft Office-based Critical Thinking exercises, you will also be utilizing various work-readiness skills, some of which are listed next to each exercise. Go to labyrinthelab.com/ workreadiness to learn more about the work-readiness skills.

5.1 Create a New Presentation

WORK-READINESS SKILLS APPLIED

- Thinking creatively
- Writing
- Interpreting and evaluating information

Green Clean is preparing for a home show at the local convention center and needs a presentation informing attendees of their services. They have asked you to create a five-slide presentation introducing Green Clean to potential new clients. Add text, clip art, and anything else you feel is appropriate for your presentation. (You choose. Suggested topics might include a sustainability project, a presentation to an organization you belong to, or a mock sales presentation.) As Green Clean's management is unsure of who will be manning the booth, they want to include speaker notes so whoever is running the booth has some additional information about the slides. Add speaker notes to at least three slides and use the Spelling command to check the spelling throughout the presentation. Save your presentation as **ct-Speaker Notes** to your Lesson 05 folder. Print the speaker notes.

5.2 Add Headers and Footers

WORK-READINESS SKILLS APPLIED

- Organizing and maintaining information
- Reasoning
- Writing

Start with the ct-Speaker Notes presentation you created in the previous exercise and save a copy of it as **ct-Headers** to your Lesson 05 folder. Add slide headers and footer to all but the title slide and include the date, custom text header, page number, and custom text footer. Save your changes and then print handouts with three slides per page. Print handouts again with six slides for page. Check all spelling once again. Which set of handouts do you think is most effective for your presentation? Why? If working in a group, discuss these questions. If working alone, type your answers in a Word document named **ct-Questions** saved to your Lesson 05 folder.

5.3 Annotate a Presentation

WORK-READINESS SKILLS APPLIED

- Speaking
- Teaching others new skills or knowledge
- Participating as a member of a team

Open the ct-Headers presentation you created in the previous exercise and save it to your Lesson 05 folder as **ct-Annotations**. Run the presentation as a slide show for a partner. Use the pen tool to emphasize something on the second slide. Use the highlighter to emphasize something on the third slide. Use a different color highlighter on the fourth slide. End the slide show and save your ink annotations. Navigate through Normal view and verify your annotations have been saved. Save your changes and then close the presentation.

Adding Multimedia to Presentations

LEARNING OBJECTIVES

After studying this lesson, you will be able to:

■ Acquire and add audio to a presentation

■ Acquire and add video to a presentation

■ Edit movies and add movie effects

■ Use slide show timings

■ Loop a presentation endlessly

Sound and movies can enhance a slide show to the point that a presentation is more than just information—it's entertaining. PowerPoint 2010 makes the development of "infotaining" presentations quick and easy. And if you don't have your own audio or video files, PowerPoint offers an extensive gallery of sounds and animated images you can use. In this lesson, you will work with PowerPoint's media features to enhance your presentations.

Adding Multimedia to the Presentation

Green Clean annually donates to a variety of charities, including animal rescue charities and young musician scholarships. Jenna, the administrative assistant, has been charged with creating a few new presentations that will play in a kiosk in the lobby at Green Clean's main office. They will showcase the animals and young musicians who have benefited from Green Clean's generosity. She wants the presentations to be entertaining and engaging, but also needs them to run by themselves with no human physically clicking through the slides. She decides to add audio and video to the presentations and to use slide timings so that they will run unattended.

The full-motion video on the slide includes audio, allowing viewers to hear and see the effects of Green Clean's charitable donations.

Video Lesson   labyrinthelab.com/videos

Multimedia, also called rich media, includes video and audio that can enhance a presentation. A presentation delivered by a photographer may play a soundtrack of classical music while the slides display a gallery of wedding photos. A presentation used to train employees may have a narration playing throughout the slideshow explaining company policy. A presentation given by a summer camp to prospective families may include videos of camp activities. Multimedia may be incorporated so simply as to play an audible *click* when navigating to subsequent slides during a presentation. Although multimedia can add excitement to your presentation, it can become overwhelming and distracting if used in excess.

Add multimedia to your presentation sparingly and only when there is true value in doing so.

Types of Multimedia

PowerPoint lets you add a variety of multimedia types to your presentation, including the following:

- **Audio:** This includes short sound effects such as a click or creaking door as well as entire songs or narration soundtracks. Most users will be familiar with MP3 or WAV sound files, but PowerPoint supports several additional types of sound files that are discussed later in this lesson.

- **Video:** This can include home movies from your camcorder or downloaded videos from the Internet. PowerPoint does not let you create the video itself. You will need to create your MPG or AVI video file in advance. Video file types and the software needed to create them are discussed later in this lesson.

- **Animated GIFs:** Animated GIFs, which are simple animated clip art images, are available through PowerPoint's Clip Art panel. There are also thousands of sources on the Internet for free animated GIF downloads.

Linked Media Files

Most multimedia files exist as separate files outside your presentation that are linked to your presentation . However, linked multimedia files function differently than linked data files such as a spreadsheet. You should already know that if a linked data file (such as an Excel spreadsheet) is moved or renamed, your presentation will not suffer. The chart will still display and you will encounter problems only if you try to edit the chart data. When a linked multimedia file is moved or renamed, it will not play during the presentation. Therefore, it is recommended you store the presentation and all linked media files in the same folder—and don't change the names of the multimedia files after they have been linked. This makes copying your presentation to other media, such as a USB drive or CD, easier as you simply copy all the files in the presentation folder to the new location.

PowerPoint does permit some types and sizes of sound files to be embedded in the presentation rather than linked. This is covered in the Using Audio in Presentations section.

Organizing Media with Subfolders

If you have many linked multimedia files, you may decide to keep your files organized in subfolders rather than having all of your files at the same level within a single folder. This makes it easier to find and launch your presentation, and makes it easier to find any multimedia files you may need to edit.

When all files are in the same folder, finding the one you need may be difficult (left). Organizing your files by type in subfolders makes it easy to find what you want when you want it (right).

DEVELOP YOUR SKILLS 6.1.1
Create Multimedia Folders (Win XP)

Win Vista/7 Users: Skip this version of the exercise and perform the steps in Develop Your Skills on page 195.

In this exercise, you will create folders to store your various types of multimedia files.

1. Choose **Start→My Computer** from the lower-left corner of your screen.

2. Navigate to the Lesson 06 folder on your file storage location.

3. Click **View** on the menu bar, and then choose **Tiles** as shown in the following image.

From here forward, menu bar commands such as the preceding one will be written Choose View→Tiles from the menu bar.

4. Choose **File→New→Folder** from the Lesson 06 folder's menu bar.

Windows displays the new folder, ready for you to type its new name.

5. Type **Audio** as the folder name and **tap** ⎡Enter⎤.

6. Repeat **steps 4** and **5** to create a second folder, but name the second folder **Video**.

7. Choose **View→Arrange Icons By→Type** from the menu bar.

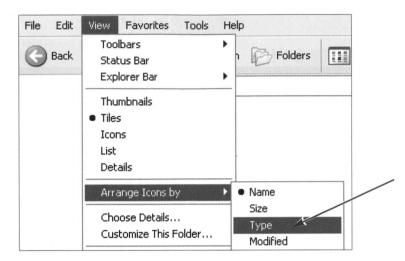

Windows sorts the files in the folder by file type. This groups audio files, video files, and so forth, so they will be easy to select and move in the next steps.

8. Follow these steps to select files to move:

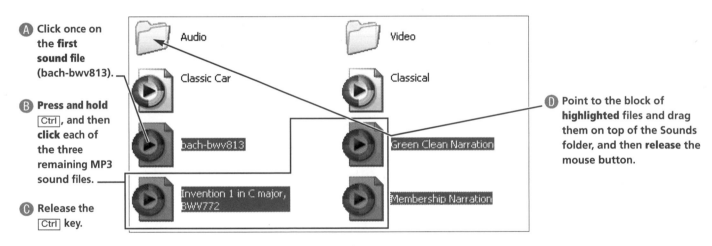

Ⓐ Click once on the **first sound file** (bach-bwv813).

Ⓑ **Press and hold** ⎡Ctrl⎤, and then **click** each of the three remaining MP3 sound files.

Ⓒ **Release the** ⎡Ctrl⎤ **key.**

Ⓓ Point to the block of **highlighted** files and drag them on top of the Sounds folder, and then **release** the mouse button.

Windows moves the four audio files to the Audio folder. Note that your icons may look different if your computer has other multimedia software installed.

9. Select the **two movie files,** Classical and Classic Cars, and move them into the **Video** folder.
Your Lesson 06 folder is now organized with multimedia subfolders.

Skip the Win Vista/7 version of this exercise and continue reading the next topic.

Create Multimedia Folders (WinVista/7)

In this exercise, you will create folders to store your various types of multimedia files.

1. Choose **Start→Computer** from the lower-left corner of your screen.

2. Navigate to the Lesson 06 folder on your file storage location.

3. Follow the steps for your version of Windows:

   ■ **Win Vista:** Choose **Views menu→Medium Icons** from the command bar.

   ■ **Win 7:** Choose **More Options→Medium Icons** from the command bar.

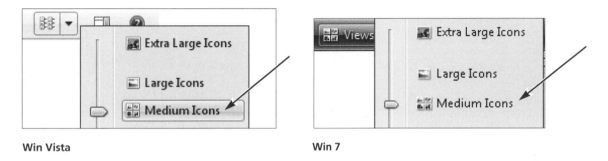

Win Vista   **Win 7**

4. Follow the steps for your version of Windows:

   ■ **Win Vista:** Choose **Organize→New Folder** from the Lesson 06 folder's command bar.

   ■ **Win 7:** Choose **New Folder** from the Lesson 06 folder's command bar.

   Windows displays the new folder, ready for you to type its new name.

Win Vista

Win 7

5. Type **Audio** as the folder name and **tap** Enter.

6. Repeat **steps 4** and **5** to create a second folder, but name the second folder **Video**.

7. Follow these steps to move the audio files to the Audio folder:

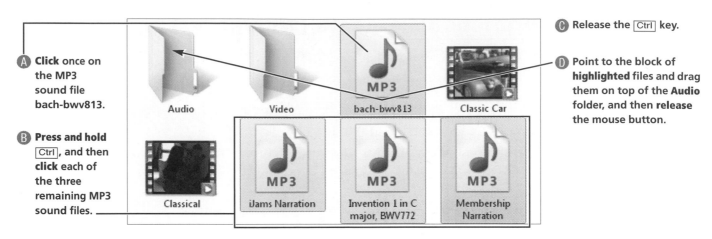

A **Click** once on the MP3 sound file bach-bwv813.

B **Press and hold** Ctrl, and then **click** each of the three remaining MP3 sound files.

C Release the Ctrl key.

D Point to the block of **highlighted** files and drag them on top of the **Audio** folder, and then **release** the mouse button.

Windows moves the four audio files to the Audio folder.

8. Select the **two movie files**, Classical and Classic Car, and move them into the **Video** folder.
   Your Lesson 06 folder is now organized with multimedia subfolders.

6.2 Using Audio in Presentations

Video Lesson   labyrinthelab.com/videos

You have many options for acquiring audio to use in a presentation. Popular sources include the following:

■ Searching for audio by keywords via the Clip Art panel

■ Ripping audio from a CD

■ Downloading an audio file from the Internet

■ Recording your own narration directly from PowerPoint or with your own software

Audio Snippets

PowerPoint comes with a library of sounds you can add to presentations. The Clip Art task pane is a great resource for finding short snippets of audio, such as a dog barking or a few bars of a musical composition. Searching for audio clips via the Clip Art task pane is similar to searching for clip art.

Audio File Types

To add an audio file to a presentation, it must be a type supported by PowerPoint. There are many types of audio formats, and PowerPoint supports the most popular ones. The following table lists the file types you can insert into a presentation.

File Type	Acronym	Filename Extension
Audio Data Transport Stream	ADTS	.adts, .adt, .aac
Audio Interchange File Format	AIFF	.aif, .aifc, .aiff
UNIX Audio	AU	.au, .snd
Musical Instrument Digital Interface	MIDI	.mid, .midi, .rmi
MPEG Audio Layer 3	MP3	.mp3, .mp2, .m3u
MPEG Audio Layer 4	MP4	.mpa
Waveform	WAV	.wav
Windows Media Audio	WMA	.wma, .wax

Adding Audio to a Presentation

Adding audio to a slide places a small speaker icon on the slide. This icon can be hidden from view during a slide show, or can function as a start/stop button for the sound. When you insert audio onto a slide, you have the option to play the sound automatically after the slide loads, or when you click the audio icon on the slide.

 Green Clean Makes a Difference

Beneficiaries of Green Clean's Generosity

A slide with a speaker icon, indicating audio has been added to the slide

Start Options

When you insert audio, PowerPoint lets you choose from three settings for playing the sound:

- **Automatically:** This setting starts playing the sound automatically when the slide loads. Navigating to the next slide automatically stops the audio.

- **On Click:** This setting starts playing the audio only when you click the speaker icon. Navigating to the next slide automatically stops the audio.

- **Play Across Slides:** This setting starts playing the audio automatically and it continues playing as you navigate to subsequent slides.

Task	Procedure
Add audio from the Clip Art panel	■ Choose Insert→Media→Audio menu→Clip Art Audio from the Ribbon to open the Clip Art panel. ■ Type your search term in the Search For box. ■ Point to one of the results, click the arrow to the right of a clip's icon, select Preview/Properties to preview the audio before adding it to your slide, and then click Close. ■ Click the clip's icon to insert it on your slide. ■ Choose Audio Tools→Playback from the Ribbon and configure how you want the audio to play.
Add audio from an external file	■ Choose Insert→Media→Audio ⊲꒾ from the Ribbon, or click the Insert Media Clip icon on the slide. ■ Browse to a supported sound file, select it, and click OK. ■ Choose Audio Tools→Playback from the Ribbon and configure how you want the audio to play.

Configuring Audio Options

When you add audio to a slide, you are immediately asked whether you would like the audio to play automatically or when clicked. If you choose to play the audio automatically, there is little reason to display the speaker icon on the slide because you no longer need to click it to play the audio. PowerPoint lets you hide the speaker icon in addition to setting a few more options, which are described in the following table.

PowerPoint lets you set a variety of options for audio in presentations.

Option	Description	How to Access
Hide During Show	Hides the speaker icon so it does not display on the slide during a slide show	■ Select the speaker icon on the slide. ■ Display Audio Tools→Playback→Audio Options from the Ribbon. ■ Check the Hide During Show checkbox.
Loop Until Stopped	Automatically plays the audio after it ends, and continues to replay it over and over until manually stopped	■ Select the speaker icon on the slide. ■ Select the Loop Until Stopped checkbox in the Audio Tools→Playback→Audio Options command group. ■ During a slide show, click the speaker icon to stop the audio.
Start	Chooses the way audio plays when you display a slide	■ Select the speaker icon on the slide. ■ Display Audio Tools→Playback→Audio Options on the Ribbon. ■ Choose the desired setting in the Start box in Audio Options. [Start: Automatically]

Playing Audio Across Multiple Slides

By default, audio plays only on the slide to which it was added. Navigating to another slide stops the audio. However, this can be changed and the audio can play across all slides in a presentation. Audio that plays across slides must start automatically when the slide containing the audio loads. For example, your presentation may include a narration or background music that begins when the first slide is displayed and continues to play for the duration of the slide show.

DEVELOP YOUR SKILLS 6.2.1
Insert an Audio Clip

In this exercise, you will insert an audio clip from the Clip Art panel.

1. **Start** PowerPoint and make sure the PowerPoint window is **maximized**.

2. **Open** the Green Clean Beneficiaries presentation from the Lesson 06 folder.

3. Follow these steps to search for audio clips:

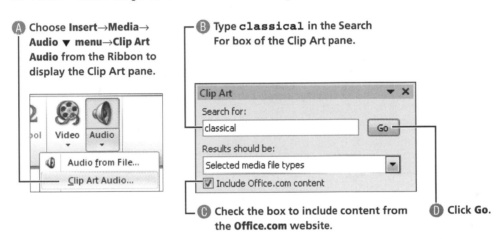

Ⓐ Choose **Insert→Media→Audio ▼ menu→Clip Art Audio** from the Ribbon to display the Clip Art pane.

Ⓑ Type **classical** in the Search For box of the Clip Art pane.

Ⓒ Check the box to include content from the **Office.com** website.

Ⓓ Click **Go**.

4. Follow these steps to preview the results and add an audio clip to your slide:

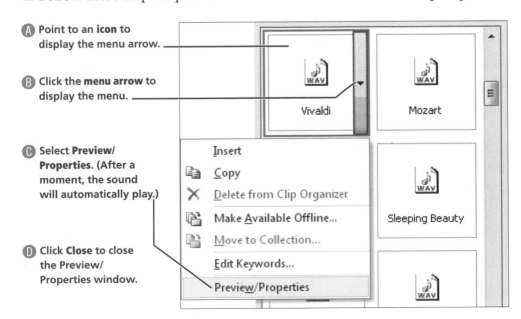

Ⓐ Point to an **icon** to display the menu arrow.

Ⓑ Click the **menu arrow** to display the menu.

Ⓒ Select **Preview/Properties**. (After a moment, the sound will automatically play.)

Ⓓ Click **Close** to close the Preview/Properties window.

5. Click the **sound icon** to insert it on the slide, or repeat the previous step to preview a different sound.

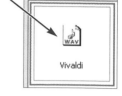

Vivaldi

6. Follow these steps to set how the audio starts:

Ⓐ Choose the **Audio Tools**→**Playback** tab from the Ribbon. If you do not see the Playback tab, click the **speaker icon** on the slide.

Ⓑ Set the Start option to **Automatically**.

7. Choose **Slide Show**→**Start Slide Show**→**From Beginning** from the Ribbon to start the slide show.
The sound starts to play immediately after the slide loads.

8. Move your mouse until the **white mouse pointer arrow** appears and then point to the **speaker icon** on the slide.
A control bar appears indicating the progress. There is also a pause button and volume control.

9. Click the **pause** button to pause the audio.

10. Move your mouse again until the **white mouse pointer arrow** appears and then point to the **speaker** icon.

11. Click the **play** button to resume the audio.

12. **Click** anywhere on the slide to advance to the next slide.
The audio stops when the presentation advances to the next slide.

13. **Tap** Esc to end the slide show and return to Normal view.

14. **Close** the Clip Art panel.

15. **Save** your presentation and continue with the next topic.

Acquiring More Audio

Video Lesson   labyrinthelab.com/videos

Copying music from a CD into a digital music file on your computer is referred to as *ripping* and can be accomplished with software such as Windows Media Player or the free Audiograbber (http://www.audiograbber.com-us.net). Windows Media Player rips to the WMA format by default, but can rip to MP3 by installing a plug-in. Audiograbber is great in that it rips directly to MP3 with no additional configuration or plug-ins, so your ripped files are already in an appropriate format to use in a presentation—and a universal format to be played outside of your presentation. Be sure you are not violating any copyright laws if ripping sound from a CD.

Downloading Sound Effects

Many websites offer audio downloads in the form of sound effect clips, music background tracks, or promotional releases for bands. The web page for this book contains links to some free sound effects websites. Again, be aware of copyright law when downloading sound files.

Links to some popular audio websites are available on the web page for this book.

Recording a Narration

If your computer has a microphone and the right software, you can record your own narration. You can use the Sound Recorder software that comes free with Windows (located at Start→ All Programs→Accessories→Entertainment→Sound Recorder for Win XP, and Start→All Programs→Accessories→Sound Recorder for Win Vista and Win 7), or purchase sound editing software such as Adobe® Audition® or Sony Sound Forge®.

Choosing an Audio File Format

Sounds from the Clip Art panel are usually in WMA or WAV format, but what if you are creating your own audio file? Whether you decide to download, purchase, rip, or record audio, you'll need to decide on the file format. Should you use a WAV file? A WMA file? An MP3 file? A MIDI file? What about AIFF or AU? Because WAV and MP3 files are the most prevalent, and every modern PC can play these without additional software or codecs, you should stick to these two file types when ripping or recording your own narration.

QUICK REFERENCE	CHOOSING AN AUDIO FILE FORMAT
File Format/ Extension	**When to Use**
.mid, .midi	▪ Use when computerized reproductions of instrumental music are desired. ▪ Use when instrumental music is needed and small file size is important.
.mp3	▪ Use for music ripped from a CD or recorded narration. *Example:* a song that plays across slides throughout the entire presentation.
.wav	▪ Use for small sound bites that are a few kilobytes in size. *Example:* a click sound or door slam effect.
.wma	▪ Use for music ripped from a CD or recorded narration. *Example:* a song that plays across slides throughout the entire presentation.

MP3 Compared to the WAV File Format

If the files are only a few kilobytes in size, it doesn't matter whether you use WAV or MP3. However, MP3 files are compressed, whereas WAV files are not. Although WAV files may sound a little better to the trained ear, an MP3 of the same sound will be about one-tenth of the file size. Most people can't tell any difference in quality between a WAV and MP3. The MP3 encoding process attempts to remove audio information that is outside the range of what humans can hear. In other words, the average person won't miss the audio that was removed from an MP3 file but will certainly notice the smaller file size.

Dancing Queen.mp3	Dancing Queen.wav	Dancing Queen.mid
MP3 Format Sound	Wave Sound	MIDI Sequence
3.54 MB	39.0 MB	68.1 KB

The same song saved as a 39 MB WAV, 3.54 MB MP3, and 68.1 KB MIDI file

The WMA Format

The WMA format is an alternative to MP3 with comparable compression and quality, but not all music player software and hardware support the WMA format.

Because the MP3 format is more universally supported, it is recommended over the WMA format.

The MIDI File Format

MIDI files also have their place and are probably the third type of sound file you are likely to use. MIDI files don't contain sound information like WAV or MP3 files. They simply provide instructions to the computer to reproduce the sounds of musical instruments. What you hear when you play a MIDI file depends on your computer's sound hardware. Your computer may really sound like a violin when you play that MIDI file of a Paganini violin concerto, whereas another computer will not sound like a true violin at all.

It is important to note that MIDI files cannot reproduce vocal tracks and should be used only when instrumental music is desired. (They are great for karaoke!)

DEVELOP YOUR SKILLS 6.2.2

Add Audio from an External File

In this exercise, you will add an audio file to a presentation and configure various options.

Add Audio to a Presentation

1. Display the **title slide**.

2. Click **once** (do not double-click) to select the speaker icon on the title slide, and then **tap** Delete to remove the sound from the slide.

3. Choose **Slide Show→Start Slide Show→From Beginning** from the Ribbon and preview the entire slide show. Return to the first slide in Normal view when you are done. *While the fading slide transitions certainly enhance the presentation, some nice music in the background would really set the mood.*

4. Choose **Insert→Media→Audio** from the Ribbon.

5. Navigate to your Lesson 06\Audio folder, select the **bach-bwv813 MP3** sound file, and click **Insert**. *Remember that your computer may be configured to hide the file extensions and the .mp3 portion of the filename may not be displayed.*

6. Choose the **Audio Tools→Playback** tab from the Ribbon and set the Start option to Automatically.

7. **Save** your presentation and continue with the next topic.

Embedding Audio

Video Lesson   labyrinthelab.com/videos

Although you can link external audio files to a presentation like other multimedia content, it is also possible to embed such files into the presentation file itself. This topic explains when you can use embedded audio.

Embedded Files

An *embedded file* is one that becomes absorbed into the presentation file itself rather than existing as a separate linked file. The obvious benefit of an embedded file is that you never have to worry about accidentally moving it or renaming it and not having it play in your presentation. The downside to using an embedded file is that it increases the file size of your presentation and is impossible to edit.

Embedded Audio Files

PowerPoint 2010, unlike previous versions of PowerPoint, allows any type of audio file to be embedded—providing the file is less than 50 MB. You can choose to embed (or link) an audio file from the Insert Audio dialog.

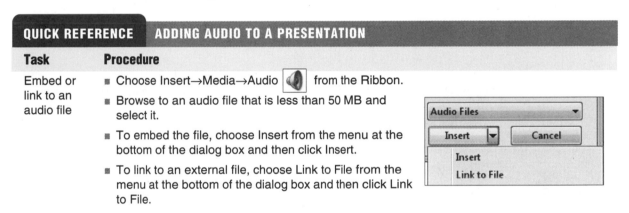

QUICK REFERENCE	ADDING AUDIO TO A PRESENTATION
Task	**Procedure**
Embed or link to an audio file	■ Choose Insert→Media→Audio 🔊 from the Ribbon. ■ Browse to an audio file that is less than 50 MB and select it. ■ To embed the file, choose Insert from the menu at the bottom of the dialog box and then click Insert. ■ To link to an external file, choose Link to File from the menu at the bottom of the dialog box and then click Link to File.

DEVELOP YOUR SKILLS 6.2.3
Break and Repair a Link to a Media File

In this exercise, you will determine whether a sound is embedded or linked. You will then purposefully break the link to a linked file to see what happens when you attempt to play the presentation. Finally, you will repair the link and confirm that the media file plays.

Before You Begin: Verify that your computer is capable of playing sound and turn up your speakers.

Determine Whether an Audio File Is Embedded or Linked

1. Choose **File→Info** from the Ribbon.

2. Locate the **Related Documents** section at the bottom of the right column of Backstage view and note the absence of a link to Related Documents.

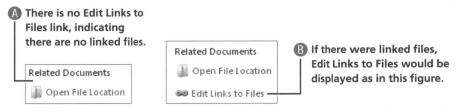

Ⓐ There is no Edit Links to Files link, indicating there are no linked files.

Ⓑ If there were linked files, Edit Links to Files would be displayed as in this figure.

3. Click the **Home** tab to exit Backstage view.

4. Click the **speaker** icon on the slide and **tap** ⬚Delete⬚ to delete the embedded audio file.

5. Choose **Insert→Media→Audio** from the Ribbon.

6. **Browse** to your Lesson 06\Audio folder.

7. Follow these steps to link to, rather than embed, the audio file:

Ⓐ Click **once** on the **bach-bwv813** file to select it.

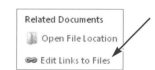

Ⓑ Click the **Insert** menu button.

Ⓒ Choose **Link to File**. The audio file is linked and is set to play On Click by default.

8. Choose **File→Info** from the Ribbon.

9. Locate the **Related Documents** section at the bottom of the right column of Backstage view and notice the Edit Links to Files link exists, indicating there are now linked files.

Related Documents
Open File Location
Edit Links to Files

10. Choose **Slide Show→Start Slide Show→From Beginning** from the Ribbon.

11. Move your mouse until the **mouse pointer white arrow** appears.

12. Point to the **speaker** icon on the slide and then click the **play** button on the control bar.
    The audio file plays.

13. **Tap** the ⬚Esc⬚ key to end the slide show and return to Normal view.

Break the Link

14. **Minimize** PowerPoint.

15. Navigate to your Lesson 06\Audio folder and locate the **bach-bwv813 MP3** file.
    If your computer is configured to display file extensions, the filename will be displayed as bach-bwv813.mp3. If your computer is configured to hide file extensions, the filename will be displayed as bach-bwv813 without any file extension.

16. **Right-click** the bach-bwv813 file and choose **Rename** from the pop-up menu.

17. Follow the appropriate instruction to rename the file:
    - If the filename is displayed as bach-bwv813 without any file extension, rename the file bach.
    - If the filename is displayed as bach-bwv813.mp3, rename the file bach.mp3, taking care not to delete the .mp3 filename extension.

18. **Maximize** PowerPoint and choose **Slide Show→Start Slide Show→From Beginning** from the Ribbon to start the slide show.

19. Move your mouse until the **mouse pointer white arrow** appears.

20. Point to the **speaker** icon on the slide and then click the **play** button on the control bar. *The audio file fails to play because the link to the file has been broken. The message* Media Unavailable *appears in the progress bar.*

21. **Tap** Esc to end the slide show and return to Normal view.

Repair the Link

22. **Minimize** PowerPoint so that you see the Lesson 06\Audio folder again.

23. Repeat **steps 16** and **17**, but rename the file back to bach-bwv813 (or bach-bwv813.mp3).

24. **Maximize** PowerPoint and choose **Slide Show→Start Slide Show→From Beginning** from the Ribbon to start the slide show.

25. Move your mouse until the **mouse pointer white arrow** appears.

26. Point to the **speaker** icon on the slide and then click the **play** button on the control bar. *The sound plays because the link has been repaired.*

27. **Tap** Esc to end the slide show and return to Normal view.

28. **Save** the presentation and continue with the next exercise.

6.3 Creating Slide Show Timings

Video Lesson	labyrinthelab.com/videos

When using background music or a narration, you often want the slide show timed to the audio so the soundtrack and slides end at the same time. Rather than guessing when to click to the next slide during a presentation, PowerPoint lets you automate the slide show by creating a slide show timing. You can even use slide show timings without audio to automatically navigate to subsequent slides during a live talk given by the presenter. As the speaker addresses the audience, the slide show can be on "autopilot," allowing the presenter to move away from the computer and interact more freely with the audience.

Determining Slide Timings

All it takes is a little math. If you can do simple division or have access to a calculator, you can time your presentation to your soundtrack and have both end at the same time. Assuming your audio begins on the first slide, and you want each slide displayed for an equal amount of time, follow these simple steps to determine the length of time to spend on each slide:

QUICK REFERENCE	DETERMINING SLIDE TIMINGS	
Task	**Procedure**	**Example**
Determine the length of the audio file in seconds	■ Select the audio icon on the slide. ■ Point to the right edge of the progress bar to see the total playing time of the audio file. ■ Convert this time to seconds.	A 2-minute 30-second audio file would be 150 seconds.
Divide the total seconds by the total slides	■ Use the Slides panel or Slide Sorter view to determine how many slides are in the presentation. ■ Divide the length of the audio in seconds by the total number of slides in the presentation.	A 150-second audio file used in a presentation containing 20 slides works out to 150 ÷ 20 = 7.5.
Determine the total time per slide	■ If your division works out to a whole number, that is the number of seconds to spend on each slide. ■ If your division works out to a decimal, you'll have to round off or use another creative solution.	The answer to the division was 7.5. You might display the first slide for 7 seconds, the next slide for 8 seconds, the next slide for 7 seconds, the next slide for 8 seconds, and so on. This averages to 7.5 seconds per slide.

Rehearsing Timings

PowerPoint's Rehearse Timings feature allows you to create an automated slide show. Use this feature to practice your speech and automatically have the slides advance as you speak, or time the presentation to a soundtrack so the audio ends just as the last slide appears.

QUICK REFERENCE	REHEARSING TIMINGS
Task	**Procedure**
Create a slide show that runs automatically	■ Choose Slide Show→Set Up→Rehearse Timings from the Ribbon. ■ Click the Next button in the Rehearsal toolbar to advance the slides. ■ When you have reached the last slide, choose Yes to save your timings or No to discard your timings.
Play a slide show with timings	■ Select the Use Timings checkbox in the Slide Show→Set Up command group.
Play a slide show manually	■ Remove the check from the Use Timings checkbox in the Slide Show→Set Up command group.

DEVELOP YOUR SKILLS 6.3.1

Apply Rehearsed Timings to a Presentation

In this exercise, you will configure the slide show to run by itself with a soundtrack.

Add Audio to a Presentation

1. Select the **speaker** icon on the title slide, and then set the **Audio Tools→Playback→ Audio Options→Start** option to **Play Across Slides**.
The sound will now start automatically and will continue to play as you navigate through the slides.

2. Point to the **right** edge of the progress bar to determine the total playing time for the audio file, as shown at right.
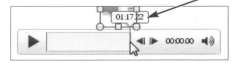
The sound is about 1 minute and 17 seconds (01:17) in length.

3. Follow these steps to calculate the length of time to spend on each slide:
   - Determine the **total number of** slides in the presentation. In this case, there are 10.
   - Determine the **length** of the sound clip in seconds. In this case, 1:17 equals 77 seconds.
   - **Divide** the length of the sound by the total number of slides. In this case, 77 ÷ 10.
   - The total amount of time to spend on each slide is about 7.7 seconds.

4. Choose **Slide Show→Set Up→Rehearse Timings** 📷 from the Ribbon and keep your eye on the timer.

5. As soon as the timer hits 7 seconds, click the **Next** button in the Rehearsal toolbar to advance to the next slide.

6. Click the **Next** button every 7 or 8 seconds, until you reach the last slide.

7. Choose **Yes** when prompted to save your timings.
   PowerPoint saves your timings and displays your slides in Slide Sorter view, where you can see the timings for each individual slide.

8. **Double-click** the first slide to display it in Normal view.

9. Select the **speaker** icon.

10. Display the **Audio Tools→Playback→Audio Options** command group from the Ribbon.

11. Place a checkmark in the **Hide During Show** option box.
    Although it's still visible now, this setting will hide the speaker icon when you display the presentation in slide show mode.

12. Choose **Slide Show→Start Slide Show→From Beginning** from the Ribbon and watch as the slide show autoplays with the soundtrack.

13. Click anywhere on the **black screen** after the slide show ends.

Loop a Slide Show

14. Choose **Slide Show→Set Up→Set Up Slide Show** from the Ribbon.

15. Place a checkmark in the **Loop Continuously Until 'Esc'** option box and click **OK**.
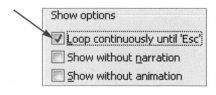

16. Choose **Slide Show→Start Slide Show→From Beginning** from the Ribbon and notice that when the last slide is reached (Corky), the slide show starts over again.

17. **Tap** [Esc] to end the slide show and return to Normal view.

18. **Save** and **close** your presentation.

6.4 Using Video in Presentations

Video Lesson   labyrinthelab.com/videos

There are two primary types of videos used in PowerPoint presentations—animated GIFs and full-motion videos. Animated GIFs are similar to clip art images, whereas full-motion videos feature true video with sound. Each of these video types are discussed in the next few paragraphs.

Searching for Videos

You have many options for acquiring videos to use in a presentation. Popular sources include the following.

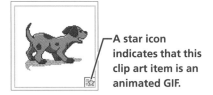

A star icon indicates that this clip art item is an animated GIF.

- Searching for videos by keywords via the Clip Art task pane. The videos found in the Clip Art pane are in the form of animated GIFs.

- Insert an existing video file you have created or down-loaded. This can include your own animated GIF or actual video.

Inserting Animated GIFs

The video clips you find with the Clip Art panel are in the form of animated GIFs. A GIF file (Graphics Interchange Format) is a type of image file format that supports simple animation like an old flip book. Imagine a stack of index cards with a slightly different picture drawn on each one. Flipping through the cards would produce a crude animation. An animated GIF is basically an electronic version of flipping through that stack of index cards. Each card in the stack of index cards is similar to a *frame* in an animated GIF. The following figure illustrates a four-frame animated GIF. When each frame is displayed for a fraction of a second, it looks like the dog is barking and wagging its tail.

Sizing Animated GIFs

Although you can resize an animated GIF image just like any other piece of clip art, it is not recommended. The regular clip art images you insert from the Clip Art panel are in a format that allows for enlarging without any loss in quality. The GIF format does not allow that. If you enlarge a GIF, it will become blurry and leave a negative impression on the attendees.

The same GIF file at its original size (above) and enlarged (right).

Add a Clip Art Video to a Presentation

In this exercise, you will add a video (animated GIF) from the Clip Art panel.

1. **Open** the Green Clean Scholarship presentation from the Lesson 06 folder.

2. Choose **Insert→Images→Clip Art** to open the Clip Art panel.

3. Follow these steps to search for an animated musical instrument:

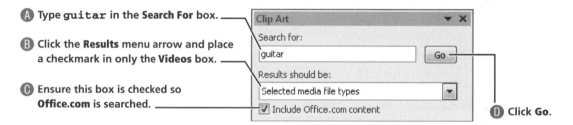

Ⓐ Type **guitar** in the **Search For** box.

Ⓑ Click the **Results** menu arrow and place a checkmark in only the **Videos** box.

Ⓒ Ensure this box is checked so **Office.com** is searched.

Ⓓ Click **Go**.

4. Follow these steps to preview the animated GIF before adding it to the slide:

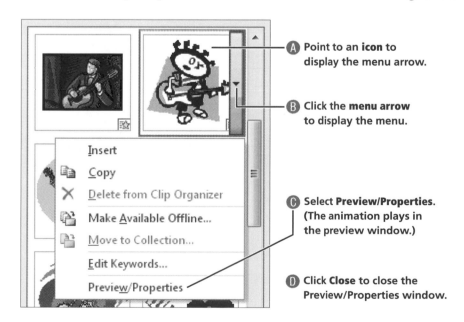

Ⓐ Point to an **icon** to display the menu arrow.

Ⓑ Click the **menu arrow** to display the menu.

Ⓒ Select **Preview/Properties**. (The animation plays in the preview window.)

Ⓓ Click **Close** to close the Preview/Properties window.

5. Click the **GIF's** thumbnail to insert it on the slide, or repeat the previous step to preview a different movie.
Your selection may differ from the illustration.

6. Drag **up** and to the **left** on the top-left handle of the movie image to enlarge it.
The image becomes blurry. Animated GIFs should not be enlarged.

7. Tap Ctrl + Z to undo the resizing of the GIF.

8. Drag the movie to the **left** of the 2010 Recipients subtitle. (Your slide may differ slightly from the following illustration.)

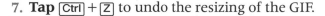

Green Clean
Young Musician Scholarships

2010 Recipients

9. Choose **Slide Show→Start Slide Show→From Beginning** to start the slide show.
The animated GIF starts playing after the slide loads.

10. Tap Esc to exit the slide show.

11. **Close** the Clip Art panel.

12. **Save** the presentation.

Inserting Videos

Video Lesson   labyrinthelab.com/videos

You can create your own full-motion video movie files with video-editing software such as the free Windows Movie Maker available for Win XP/Vista/7 or third-party software such as Studio™ made by Pinnacle (www.pinnaclesys.com). You can also download videos from the Internet. Animated GIFs can be inserted from the Clip Art panel or downloaded from the Internet.

As with audio files, be sure you are not violating any copyright laws when downloading and using videos in a presentation. Always check a website's Terms and Conditions before using any downloaded multimedia content.

QUICK REFERENCE	ADDING MOVIES TO A PRESENTATION
Task	**Procedure**
Add a video from the Clip Art panel	■ Choose Insert→ Images→Clip Art from the Ribbon to open the Clip Art panel. ■ Type your search term and select the Videos option from the Results Should Be menu. ■ Click the arrow to the right of a clip's icon and select Preview/Properties to preview the video before adding it to your slide, and then click Close. ■ Click the clip's icon to insert it on your slide.
Add videos from an existing external file	■ Choose Insert→Media→Video from the Ribbon, or click the Insert Media Clip icon on the slide. ■ Browse to a supported video file, select it, and click OK. ■ Choose to start the video automatically, or when the video is clicked.
Change settings for a video	■ Select the video placeholder on the slide. ■ Choose the Video Tools→Playback contextual tab on the Ribbon. ■ Configure or change settings from the Video Options command group.

Video File Formats

Full-motion video, like a home movie of your trip to the beach, manifests in several file formats such as MPEG or AVI. MPEG files are generally smaller files compared to AVIs and are less problematic when playing on different computers. AVI files can be problematic because of missing codecs, as explained in the next section.

QUICK REFERENCE	USING SUPPORTED VIDEO FILE TYPES

Video Format	**Acronym**	**File Extension**
Adobe Flash Media	SWF	.swf
Advanced Streaming Format	ASF	.asf, .asx, .wpl, .wm, .wmx, .wmd, .wmz, .dvr-ms
Audio Video Interleave	AVI	.avi
Moving Picture Experts Group	MPG	.mpeg, .mpg, .mpe, .m1v, .m2v, .mod, .mpv2, .mp2v, .mpa
MP4 Video	MP4	.mp4, .mp4v, .3gp, .3gpp, .3g2, .3gp2
MPEG-2 TS Video	MPEG-2	.m2ts, .m2t, .mts, .ts, .tts
QuickTime Movie	MOV	.mov
Windows Media Video	WMV	.wmv, .wvx

Codecs

Although you may think you're doing everything correctly by using a file with a supported file extension, your audio or video files may not play when the presentation is viewed on someone else's computer. This is most often due to a *codec* incompatibility.

The Role of Codecs

Audio and video multimedia files can be huge—sometimes several gigabytes. Software called a *compressor* is used to compress the file and make it smaller. To play the file, it needs to be decompressed or decoded—the job of more software called a *decompressor*. A codec, which is an abbreviation of **co**mpressor/**dec**ompressor, does both jobs.

If a multimedia file was created with a certain codec, that codec must be present on any computer wanting to successfully play the file. To confuse matters, many different codecs can create files with the same file extension, and they may not be compatible. For example, the I263, DivX, and XVID codecs all create movie files with the .avi file extension.

Identifying a Codec

Don't assume that just because an AVI video file plays on your computer, it will also play on your friend's. Your computer may have the correct codec installed while your friend's does not. This becomes an issue when using multimedia files compressed with codecs other than what Windows has installed by default—and is more of an issue with video than with audio. Software such as MediaInfo or AVIcodec—both free—can identify what codec is needed to play a certain video file.

See the web page for this book for links to useful codec utilities such as the ones mentioned in the preceding paragraph.

Figuring Out a Codec

You will find videos with nonstandard codecs very often with AVI files downloaded from the Internet. Also, some video-editing software may use nonstandard codecs when creating AVI files. The best advice is to simply try to play the video with Windows Media Player before inserting it in your presentation. If it plays in Windows Media Player, it will play in your presentation. If it fails to play, identify the codec by using software such as MediaInfo or AVIcodec. Then search the Internet for the codec, download it, and install it. The website VideoHelp.com is an excellent source for learning more about video and video codecs and offers a Tools section where you can download codecs and other helpful software.

When a Codec Is Missing

If you attempt to run a slide show with a multimedia file for which you do not have the correct codec, you will not receive any error. The media file will simply not play.

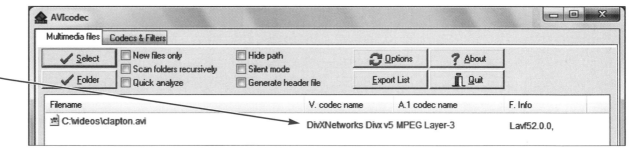

The AVIcodec software has identified the DivX codec in the dog_training.avi movie.

Always make sure that your presentation computer has the necessary codecs for any movie to be played in your presentation.

Task	Procedure
Determine whether there is a problem	■ Attempt to play an AVI file with Windows Media Player. ■ If it plays, there is no problem with a missing codec. ■ If it fails to play or you receive a "missing codec" error message, proceed with the next steps to identify and install the missing codec.
Identify the codec	■ Use a program such as AVIcodec to identify what codec was used to compress the video. ■ A link to the AVIcodec website appears on the web page for this book.
Install the missing codec	■ Search the Internet for the codec identified in the previous step. Usually typing the name of the codec in a search engine provides the results you need.

Google

divx codec

Advanced search
Language tools

Google Search   I'm Feeling Lucky

■ Download the codec installer to an easy-to-find location, such as your Desktop.

■ Be sure you are running current antivirus software, antispyware software, and are downloading the codec from a reputable source!

■ Double-click the downloaded file and follow the onscreen instructions to install the codec. Note that you may need to reboot your computer after installing.

■ Attempt to play the video again.

DEVELOP YOUR SKILLS 6.4.2

Insert a Video into a Presentation

In this exercise, you will add a video from an existing external file.

1. Choose **Home→Slides→New Slide** from the Ribbon and type **Scholarship Recipient** as a title.

2. Click the **Insert Media Clip** icon on the slide.

3. Navigate to your Lesson 06\Video folder, select the **Classical MPEG** video movie file, and click **Insert** to embed the video.
   Your computer may be configured to hide file extensions and may not display the .mpg portion of the filename. The video is added to the slide and is set to play on click by default.

4. Choose **Slide Show→Start Slide Show→From Beginning** from the Ribbon to start the slide show.

5. Notice the animated GIF on the title slide, and then **click** anywhere to advance to the next slide.

6. Move your mouse around until the **mouse pointer** becomes visible.

7. Point to the **video** to display the control bar at the bottom and click the **play** button to start the video.
   Point to the video again to display the control bar and use the play/pause button to pause or resume the video.

8. When the movie ends, **tap** [Esc] to return to Normal view.
   You may have heard a clicking sound at the beginning and end of the video—a sound the video camera itself made. You will remove unwanted sounds such as this in the next exercise.

9. **Save** 🔲 your presentation and continue with the next topic.

Editing Videos

Video Lesson   labyrinthelab.com/videos

New to PowerPoint 2010 is the ability to edit videos. While PowerPoint is not meant to replace a full video-editing suite, it offers basic editing functions. You can trim the start and end of a video (cut off the beginning or the end) and have it fade in or out. All of these options are available on the contextual Video Tools→Playback tab.

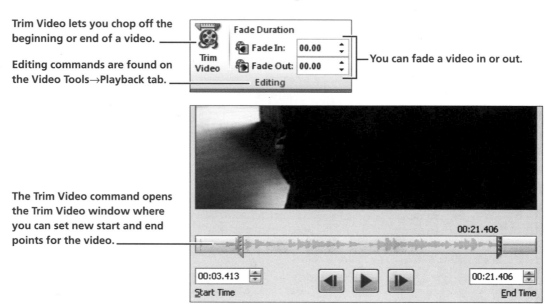

Trim Video lets you chop off the beginning or end of a video.

Editing commands are found on the Video Tools→Playback tab.

You can fade a video in or out.

The Trim Video command opens the Trim Video window where you can set new start and end points for the video.

Video Effects

Also new to PowerPoint 2010 is the ability to apply video effects. Using the Video Styles gallery, you can easily format a video much like clip art.

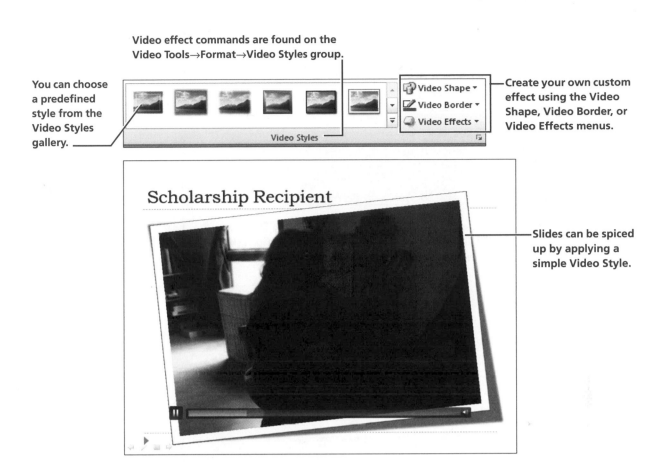

Video effect commands are found on the
Video Tools→Format→Video Styles group.

You can choose
a predefined
style from the
Video Styles
gallery.

Create your own custom
effect using the Video
Shape, Video Border, or
Video Effects menus.

Video Shape ▾
Video Border ▾
Video Effects ▾

Video Styles

Scholarship Recipient

Slides can be spiced
up by applying a
simple Video Style.

Edit and Style a Video

In this exercise, you will trim a video. You will then apply a Video Style.

Trim a Video

1. Select the **second slide**, if necessary, and click the **video** to select it.

2. Choose **Video Tools→Playback→Editing→Trim Video** 🎞 from the Ribbon.
   The Trim Video window appears.

3. Follow these steps to trim the start of the video to eliminate the popping sounds:

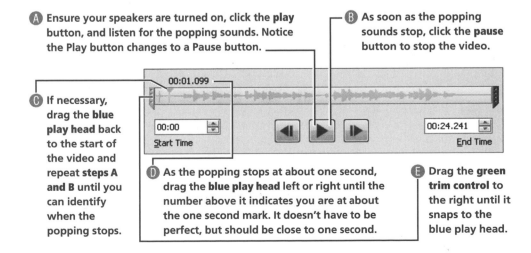

Ⓐ Ensure your speakers are turned on, click the **play** button, and listen for the popping sounds. Notice the Play button changes to a Pause button.

Ⓑ As soon as the popping sounds stop, click the **pause** button to stop the video.

Ⓒ If necessary, drag the **blue play head** back to the start of the video and repeat **steps A and B** until you can identify when the popping stops.

Ⓓ As the popping stops at about one second, drag the **blue play head** left or right until the number above it indicates you are at about the one second mark. It doesn't have to be perfect, but should be close to one second.

Ⓔ Drag the **green trim control** to the right until it snaps to the blue play head.

00:01.099

00:00 — Start Time

00:24.241 — End Time

4. Follow these steps to trim the end of the video:

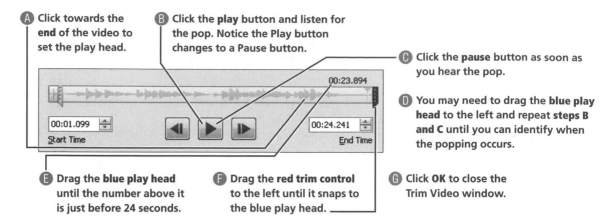

Ⓐ Click towards the **end** of the video to set the play head.

Ⓑ Click the **play** button and listen for the pop. Notice the Play button changes to a Pause button.

Ⓒ Click the **pause** button as soon as you hear the pop.

Ⓓ You may need to drag the **blue play head** to the left and repeat **steps B and C** until you can identify when the popping occurs.

Ⓔ Drag the **blue play head** until the number above it is just before 24 seconds.

Ⓕ Drag the **red trim control** to the left until it snaps to the blue play head.

Ⓖ Click **OK** to close the Trim Video window.

Apply a Video Style

5. Choose **Video Tools→Format→Video Styles→More** ▾ from the Ribbon to display the Video Styles gallery.

6. Point to several styles to see them temporarily applied to the video on the slide, then click the **Intense→Monitor, Gray style** (the third one in the bottom row). Your slide should resemble the following figure:

Scholarship Recipient

7. Choose **Slide Show→Start Slide Show→From Current Slide** from the Ribbon to start the slide show from the second slide.
   The slide displays the video with the three-dimensional style.

8. Move your mouse until the **mouse pointer white arrow** appears.

9. Point to the **video** on the slide and then click the **play** button on the control bar.

   The popping sounds at the beginning and end of the video are no longer there because the video has been trimmed.

10. **Tap** ⟨Esc⟩ to exit the slide show and return to Normal view.

11. **Save** your presentation and continue with the next topic.

Setting Video Options

Video Lesson   labyrinthelab.com/videos

Just as with audio there are several options you can apply to videos on a slide. These are available from the Video Tools→Playback-→Video Options command group.

- **Start:** You can choose to automatically start the video when the slide loads, or require the video or play button in the control bar to be clicked in order to play.

- **Hide While Not Playing:** You can hide the video placeholder during a slide show. However, this will make it impossible to click the video to start it! Use this option when Start is set to Automatically. When the video ends, it disappears (hides) so your slide doesn't display a rectangular placeholder.

- **Play Full Screen:** You can have the video play in full-screen mode, as shown in the following figure. When set to full-screen mode, the video appears as normal on the slide but enlarges to fill the screen when played. When the video is done, the size automatically reduces and the entire slide is once again visible.

- **Loop Until Stopped:** The video can be configured to rewind and start over again and again until manually stopped.

- **Rewind After Playing:** This is helpful when you want to play the video only once, but have it ready to start playing from the beginning again when clicked.

- **Volume:** Just as the name indicates, you can set the volume for the audio playback of a video. This option sets the initial volume, which can be overridden by your computer speakers' volume control.

The same slide with a video playing normally (left) and full screen (right).

Choosing the Options

There is no "wrong" or "right" when configuring these options. They are dependent on personal preference and the needs and expectations of the audience. For example, if your presentation were to play in a trade-show kiosk in a continuous loop to draw in a crowd, you would probably want video and audio to start automatically rather than requiring an icon to be clicked in order to start playback.

DEVELOP YOUR SKILLS 6.4.4
Set Video Playback Options

In this exercise, you will configure a video to play in full-screen mode.

1. Select **slide 2**, Scholarship Recipient and select the existing movie on the slide, if necessary.

2. Choose **Video Tools→Playback→Video Options** from the Ribbon.
   Windows displays the current options for the selected movie.

3. Place a checkmark in the **Play Full Screen** checkbox.

4. Choose **Slide Show→Start Slide Show→From Beginning** to start the slide show.

5. Navigate to the **second slide** and move your mouse around until the pointer becomes visible.

6. **Click** the movie to play it.
   The movie plays in full-screen mode. When the movie is done, it returns to normal size and the slide is visible again.

7. **Tap** Esc to end the slide show.

8. **Save** 🖫 and **close** your presentation.

6.5 Concepts Review

Concepts Review   labyrinthelab.com/pp10

To check your knowledge of the key concepts introduced in this lesson, complete the Concepts Review quiz by going to the URL listed above. If your classroom is using Labyrinth eLab, you may complete the Concepts Review quiz from within your eLab course.

Reinforce Your Skills

Add an Animated GIF

In this exercise, you will add an animated GIF to the Blue Mountain Realty Featured Homes presentation.

1. **Open** the sb-Featured Homes presentation from your Lesson 06 folder.

2. Choose **Insert→Images→Clip Art** from the Ribbon to display the Clip Art panel.

3. Follow these steps to search for an animated GIF:

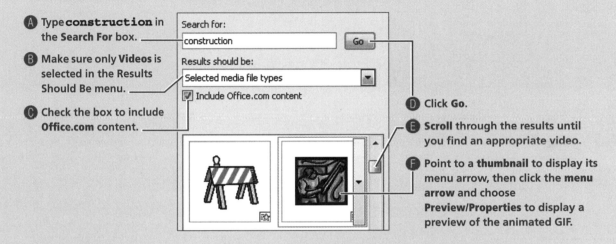

Ⓐ Type **construction** in the **Search For** box.

Ⓑ Make sure only **Videos** is selected in the Results Should Be menu.

Ⓒ Check the box to include **Office.com** content.

Search for:

construction   Go

Results should be:

Selected media file types ▾

☑ Include Office.com content

Ⓓ Click **Go**.

Ⓔ **Scroll** through the results until you find an appropriate video.

Ⓕ Point to a **thumbnail** to display its menu arrow, then click the **menu arrow** and choose **Preview/Properties** to display a preview of the animated GIF.

4. Close the **Preview/Properties** window.

5. Click the **thumbnail** to insert the animated GIF on the slide, or continue to preview others until you find one you like.

6. Drag the **video** to the desired location on the slide. Remember not to resize the video—it will become blurry.

7. Choose **Slide Show→Start Slide Show→From Beginning**.
   The slide show starts and the animated GIF plays.

8. **Tap** [Esc] to end the slide show and return to Normal view.

9. **Close** the Clip Art panel.

10. **Save** your presentation and continue with the next exercise.

Add Sound to Play Across Slides

In this exercise, you will add a musical background to the presentation.

Add Audio to a Slide

1. Display the **title slide** if necessary.

2. Choose **Insert→Media→Audio** from the Ribbon.

3. Browse to the Lesson 06\Audio folder.

4. Follow these steps to add the audio to your presentation:

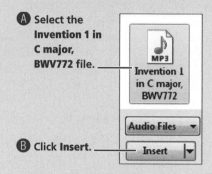

Ⓐ Select the Invention 1 in C major, BWV772 file.

Ⓑ Click **Insert**.

Configure the Audio to Play Across All Slides

5. Click the **speaker** on the slide if necessary and choose **Audio Tools→Playback→Audio Options→Start→Play Across Slides** from the Ribbon.

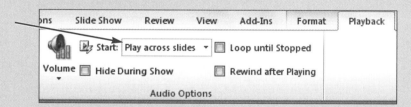

Test the Audio

6. Choose **Slide Show→Start Slide Show→From Beginning** from the Ribbon to start the slide show.

7. **Click** through the slide show until it ends, and then return to Normal view.

8. **Save** your presentation and continue with the next exercise.

Apply Rehearsed Timings

In this exercise, you will automate the slide show and time it to the soundtrack.

Determine the Sound Length

1. Display the **title slide** if necessary.

2. Follow these steps to determine the playing length of the audio:

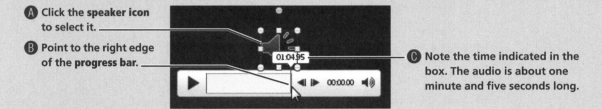

Ⓐ Click the **speaker icon** to select it.

Ⓑ Point to the right edge of the **progress bar**.

Ⓒ Note the time indicated in the box. The audio is about one minute and five seconds long.

Determine Slide Timings

3. Follow these steps to determine the amount of time to spend on each slide:

   ■ Scroll to the bottom of the **Slides** panel to see there are nine slides in the presentation then scroll back to the top.

   ■ Convert the audio length, 1:05, to **seconds** (65 seconds).

   ■ **Divide** the audio length by the number of slides. 65 ÷ 9 = 7.222… So each slide should display for about seven seconds.

4. Choose **Slide Show→Set Up→Rehearse Timings** and follow these steps to time the slides:

Ⓐ Watch the timer until it shows **0:00:07**.

Ⓑ Click the **Next** button to advance to the next slide.

Ⓒ When the timer displays 0:00:14, click **Next** again.

Ⓓ Continue to advance the slides every **seven seconds** until the slide show ends.

5. Choose **Yes** when asked whether you want to save the timings.

Finalize the Settings

6. **Double-click** the first slide to return to Normal view.

7. Click the **speaker** icon to select it.

8. Choose **Audio Tools→Playback→Audio Options→Hide During Show** to hide the speaker icon during a slide show.

9. Choose **Slide Show→Set Up→Set Up Slide Show** from the Ribbon.

10. Select the Loop **Continuously Until 'Esc'** checkbox and click **OK**.

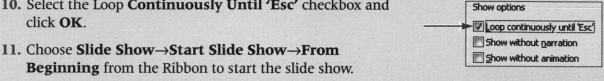

11. Choose **Slide Show→Start Slide Show→From Beginning** from the Ribbon to start the slide show.

12. Watch the slide show as it auto-advances to each slide. Wait until the last slide is displayed and the slide show automatically starts over again, and then **tap** [Esc] to end the slide show.

13. **Save** your presentation.

Apply Your Skills

Add Audio to an Automated Presentation

In this exercise, you will add an audio narration and have it play across all slides in an automated presentation.

Add Audio

1. **Open** the as-Classic Cars presentation from your Lesson 06 folder.

2. Insert the **Membership Narration** audio file from your Lesson 06 folder onto the title slide.

3. Set the audio to play across **all slides**.

4. Hide the **speaker icon** so it does not display during a slide show.

Set Timings

5. Use the following settings to set up Rehearsed Timings:

Slide	Seconds to stay on slide
Title slide	5
2,000,000 + Members	12
Apply Now	9
Free Magazine	10
Web Access	8
Auctions	10
Last Slide	20

The audio will end on the Auctions slide. You are displaying the last slide for 20 additional seconds (of silence), as a video clip will be placed on that slide in the next exercise.

6. **Run** the slide show and ensure the slides auto-advance and the audio matches the slide. If there are problems, redo the slide timings.

7. **Save** your presentation and continue with the next exercise.

Add and Format a Video

In this exercise, you will add and format a video clip.

1. Return to **Normal** view and display the **last slide**, if necessary.

2. Click the **Media** icon in the left placeholder and insert the **Classic Car** video from your Lesson 06 folder.

3. Set the video to start **automatically**.

4. Use the **Video Tools→Format→Video Styles** commands to format the video. The figure below shows one possible example:

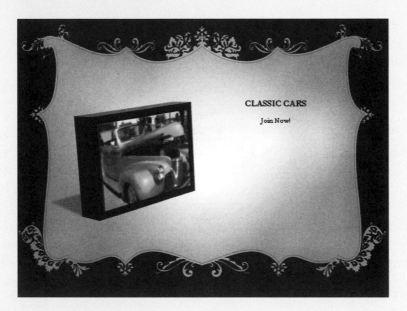

5. **Run** the slide show from the beginning and verify the video starts automatically when the last slide is displayed.

6. When the slide show ends, return to **Normal** view.

7. **Save** and **close** your presentation.

Critical Thinking &
Work-Readiness Skills

In the course of working through the following Microsoft Office-based Critical Thinking exercises, you will also be utilizing various work-readiness skills, some of which are listed next to each exercise. Go to labyrinthelab.com/ workreadiness to learn more about the work-readiness skills.

6.1 Create a Nature Presentation

As a Green Clean representative, you have been asked to create a presentation showcasing the beauty of the earth. Create at least seven slides and insert a nature photograph on every slide. You might use PowerPoint's clip art command to search for nature photographs, or find your own photos some other way. Search the Internet for **public domain music** and find appropriate background music for your slide slow. Insert the audio file on the title slide and configure it to play automatically at start across all slides. Add a speaker note on the title slide indicating the URL you used to download the audio file. Save your presentation as **ct-Nature Slides** to your Lesson 06 folder. If working in a group, discuss why Green Clean might create such a slide show, what business purposes it might address. If working alone, type your answers in a Word document named **ct-Questions** saved to your Lesson 06 folder.

WORK-READINESS SKILLS APPLIED

- Thinking creatively
- Seeing things in the mind's eye
- Making decisions

6.2 Add Slide Show Timings to a Presentation

Start with the ct-Nature Slides presentation you created in the previous exercise and save a copy of it with the name **ct-Nature Auto Pilot** to your Lesson 06 folder. Apply slide show timings so the slides advance automatically and the last slide appears as the audio ends. Set the slide show to repeat automatically until stopped. Save your changes. Have another student run your slide show to verify the timings are effective. If working in a group, discuss possible business uses of such an automated slide show. If working alone, type your answers in a Word document named **ct-Questions2** saved to your Lesson 06 folder.

WORK-READINESS SKILLS APPLIED

- Thinking creatively
- Seeing things in the mind's eye
- Participating as a member of a team

6.3 Add Video to a Presentation

Open the ct-Nature Auto Pilot presentation you created in the previous exercise and save it to your Lesson 06 folder with the name **ct-Nature Video**. Download a public domain nature video from the Internet and add it to a new final slide. Add a speaker note indicating the URL you used to download the video. Disable the slide show timings and looping. Trim the video, if necessary, to adjust the start and stop times. Apply a video effect. Test the slide show and save your changes.

WORK-READINESS SKILLS APPLIED

- Seeing things in the mind's eye
- Thinking creatively
- Applying technology to a task

Using Tables in Presentations

LEARNING OBJECTIVES

After studying this lesson, you will be able to:

- Insert tables and add or delete rows and columns
- Format tables and cells
- Add nontext data over cells

Until now, you have been dealing mostly with bulleted text on slides. Quite often you will need to display tabular data—that is, text inside a table. In this lesson, you will work with tables. PowerPoint has tools to easily create and format tables. It also offers professionally designed, preformatted color schemes that match your document theme. A variety of custom colors and 3-D effects can be applied to your tables, allowing you total control over the look and feel of your slides.

Creating Tables in Presentations

The last Sunday of every month, Green Clean sponsors a family picnic complete with games and live entertainment. Tommy Choi, Green Clean's president, feels it's a way to give back to the community and bond with his staff and clients. His administrative assistant, Jenna, has the responsibility of creating a presentation to show during the awards ceremony after the various picnic game competitions. She has a short time to complete these monthly presentations, because she typically creates them on her laptop computer during the post-game picnic dinner. She uses PowerPoint tables to present the day's events and competition results.

EVENTS

Team Competitions		
Egg Toss	Tommy & Mary Derek & Isabella Ken & D'Andre	
Three-Legged Race	Tommy & Talos Derek & Ken Mary & D'Andre	
Wheelbarrow Race	Isabella & Talos Derek & Mary Ken & D'Andre	
Water Balloon Toss	Tommy & Derek Ken & Mary Isabella & D'Andre	

This three-column table is formatted to match the presentation theme and lays out the day's competitions.

7.1 Using PowerPoint Tables

Video Lesson   labyrinthelab.com/videos

Tables are useful for organizing information into rows and columns. PowerPoint has table layout features that make inserting tables into slides easy. After you insert a table, you can use various manual and automatic commands to format it, change column and row sizes, and make other adjustments.

An example of a table on a PowerPoint slide

Inserting Tables

You can insert tables into slides with the table icon present on most slide layouts, or via the Ribbon. When you insert a new table, PowerPoint lets you specify the number of rows and columns it should contain.

QUICK REFERENCE	INSERTING TABLES
Task	**Procedure**
Insert a table from a slide icon	▪ Click the Insert Table 🔲 icon if present on your slide layout.
	▪ Enter the number of columns and rows desired, and click OK.
Insert a table from the Ribbon	▪ Choose Insert→Tables→Table ▼ from the Ribbon.
	▪ Drag with the mouse to visually indicate the number of rows and columns desired for the table, and then release the mouse button.

Create a PowerPoint Table

In this exercise, you will create a PowerPoint table.

1. **Start** PowerPoint, **maximize** the program window, and **open** the Green Clean Picnic presentation from your Lesson 07 folder.

2. Select the **title slide**, and then choose **Home→Slides→New Slide** from the Ribbon.

3. In the Title placeholder, type **Events**.

4. Click the **Insert Table** icon in the center of the slide, as shown at right.
   The Insert Table dialog box appears.

5. Enter **2** for the number of columns and **6** for the number of rows, and then click **OK**.
   PowerPoint creates a table with two columns and six rows on the slide. The table is already formatted with the color scheme of the document theme. You will enter data in the table in the next exercise.

6. **Save** 💾 your presentation and continue with the next topic.

Entering Data in Tables

Video Lesson	labyrinthelab.com/videos

When you type text in a table cell, PowerPoint wraps the text to fit the cell. The cell height increases to accommodate the wrapped text. You can add text or numbers in table cells. You cannot insert pictures, clip art, other tables, SmartArt, or charts directly into a table cell. However, you will see how to accomplish a similar effect later in this chapter.

Navigating Table Cells

After inserting a new table on a slide, you will often want to enter information in each cell. Although you can click in the first cell, type your information, and then click in the next cell, type, click in the next, type, and so on, this method is not efficient because it requires you to move your hands away from the keyboard to use the mouse. Navigating table cells with the keyboard is a more efficient way to enter data initially.

QUICK REFERENCE	NAVIGATING TABLE CELLS WITH THE KEYBOARD
Task	**Procedure**
Use Tab key	■ Tap Tab to move to the next cell in the current row.
	■ If the cursor is already in the last cell in the row, tap Tab to move to the first cell in the next row.
	■ If the cursor is in the bottom-right table cell, tap Tab to create a new bottom row with the cursor in the first cell of the new row.
	■ Tap Shift + Tab to move backward through the table cells.
	■ You cannot use Shift + Tab to create new rows.
Use arrow keys	■ Tap the ←, →, ↑, ↓ arrow keys to navigate cells.
	■ You cannot use the arrow keys to create new rows.

Enter Data into a PowerPoint Table

In this exercise, you will enter data into a PowerPoint table.

Before You Begin: The Green Clean Picnic presentation should be open.

1. **Click** in the first cell of the first row and type **Team Competitions**.

2. **Tap** the ↓ key once to move the insertion point to the first cell in the second row, and then type **Egg Toss**.

3. **Tap** the Tab key to move to the next cell and **type** the following:

   Tommy & Mary [Enter]
   Derek & Isabella [Enter]
   Ken & D'Andre

4. **Tap** the Tab key and type **Three-Legged Race** in the first cell of the third row.

5. **Tap** the Tab key to move to the next cell and **type** the following:

   Tommy & Talos [Enter]
   Derek & Ken [Enter]
   Mary & D'Andre

6. **Tap** the Tab key to move to the next row, type **Wheelbarrow Race**, tap Tab, and **type** the names of the contestants in the next cell:

   Isabella & Talos [Enter]
   Derek & Mary [Enter]
   Ken & D'Andre

7. Complete the bottom two rows to match the following figure.

Water Balloon Toss	Tommy & Derek Ken & Mary Isabella & D'Andre
Piggyback Race	Mary & Isabella D'Andre & Talos Ken & Tommy

8. **Save** 💾 your presentation and continue with the next topic.

Formatting Data in Cells

Video Lesson   labyrinthelab.com/videos

Table cells and their contents can be formatted in one of two ways—character formatting or cell formatting. *Character formatting* applies only to the selected text, whereas *cell formatting* applies to all text in the cell and any future text that is typed in the cell.

Character formatting is helpful when you wish to emphasize a single word or phrase. Cell formatting is helpful when you want all the text in a cell to look the same.

In the following figure, character formatting was applied to the word *Winners*, so only that word was affected. (A larger font size was applied.) Additionally, cell format-

ting was applied to color the text white so that any new text typed in the cell is automatically formatted as white.

Aligning and Formatting Cell Entries

Alignment is one form of cell formatting. You can align the contents of cells horizontally (side to side) and vertically (top to bottom). You can also add background color, textures, or pictures to tables or cells. You will learn more about this in the next topic.

You can align the contents of table cells horizontally and vertically.

QUICK REFERENCE	SELECTING TABLE CELLS
Task	**Procedure**
Select a single cell	■ Click once inside the cell. *or* ■ Point to the left border of a cell until the mouse pointer changes to a thick diagonal arrow, and then click to select the cell.

Three-Legged Race

Wheelbarrow Race

Select multiple cells	■ Point to any cell, and then drag to any other cell. *or* ■ Click in any cell, press Shift, click in any other cell, and then release Shift.
Select columns	■ Point to the top of the table above any column until the mouse pointer turns into a thick down arrow, and then click to select a single column. ■ Point to the top of the table above any column until the mouse pointer turns into a thick down arrow, and then click and drag across to select multiple columns. ■ Click in any cell, and then choose Table Tools→Layout→Table→Select→Select Column from the Ribbon to select a single column.
Select rows	■ Point to the left of the table next to any row until the mouse pointer turns into a thick right arrow, and then click to select a single row. ■ Point to the left of the table next to any row until the mouse pointer turns into a thick right arrow, and then click and drag up or down to select multiple rows. ■ Click in any cell, and then choose Table Tools→Layout→Table→Select→Select Row from the Ribbon to select a single row.

Select Cells and Format Cell Content

In this exercise, you will select cells and apply character formatting and cell formatting.

Apply Character Formatting

1. **Double-click** the word *Egg* in the first cell of the second row.

2. Choose **Home→Font→Font Color ▾→Red** from the Ribbon.
   Only the selected word turns red.

3. **Click** once to the right of the word *Toss* in the same cell, **tap** the [Spacebar], and type **Contest**.
   The word Contest *is not red because character formatting applies only to the selected text.*

4. **Tap** [Backspace] repeatedly until the word *Contest* is deleted.

Apply Cell Formatting

5. Follow these steps to format the cell:

Ⓐ Point to the **bottom-left corner** of the cell until your mouse pointer becomes a thick diagonal arrow, and then **click** to select the cell.

Ⓑ Point to the faded mini **format bar** that is slightly visible over the cell so that it becomes fully visible.

Ⓒ Click the **Font Color menu ▾** button.

Ⓓ Choose the fourth themed color, **Pink Text 2**.

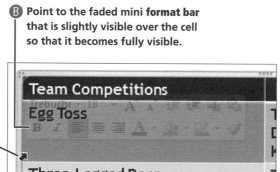

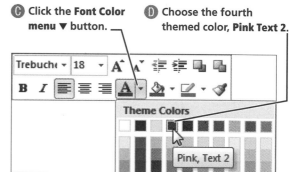

Ⓔ Move your **mouse pointer** to the bottom-right corner of the slide until the mini formatting bar disappears.

All text in the cell turns pink.

6. **Click** once to the right of the word *Toss* in the same cell, **tap** the [Spacebar], and type **Contest**.
   The word Contest *is automatically pink because cell formatting has been applied to the cell.*

7. **Tap** [Backspace] repeatedly until the word *Contest* is deleted.

8. Point to the left of the **Egg Toss** row until your mouse pointer turns into a thick right arrow.

9. Drag down to the **Piggyback Race** row and then release the mouse button.
   All but the top row becomes selected.

10. Choose **Home→Font→Font Color ▾ menu→Dark Red** from the Ribbon.

11. **Click** anywhere outside the table to deselect the highlighted rows.

12. Follow these steps to apply additional formatting to the cells:

A Point to the **Egg Toss** cell, and then drag straight down to the **Piggyback Race** cell to select five cells in the first column.

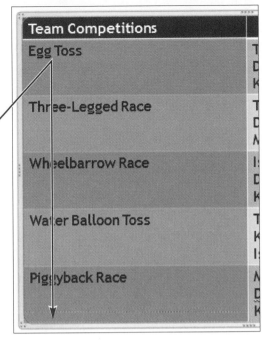

B Choose **Table Tools→Layout→ Alignment→ Align Text Right** from the Ribbon.

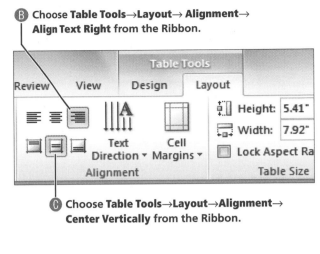

C Choose **Table Tools→Layout→Alignment→ Center Vertically** from the Ribbon.

The text in all five cells shifts to the right vertical centers of their cells.

13. Choose **Table Tools→Layout→Alignment→Align Bottom** from the Ribbon.

The text in all five cells shifts to the bottoms of their cells.

14. Choose Table **Tools→Layout→Alignment→Align Top** from the Ribbon to return the text to the top of their cells.

15. Click anywhere outside the table to deselect the highlighted cells.

16. Save 🖫 your presentation and continue with the next topic.

Adjusting Column Widths and Row Heights

Video Lesson labyrinthelab.com/videos

Depending on the design of your presentation and your own personal preference, you may want to reduce the amount of extra space in a column or row by reducing the width of a column or the height of a row. You may also want to expand the width or height to create breathing room between cells. These adjustments can be made manually or automatically. Another option is to have all the columns or all the rows equally sized and spaced.

Team Competitions	
Egg Toss	Tommy & Mary Derek & Isabella Ken & D'Andre
Three-Legged Race	Tommy & Talos Derek & Ken Mary & D'Andre
Wheelbarrow Race	Isabella & Talos Derek & Mary Ken & D'Andre

Unequal column widths and row heights make the table unbalanced.

Team Competitions	
Egg Toss	Tommy & Mary Derek & Isabella Ken & D'Andre
Three-Legged Race	Tommy & Talos Derek & Ken Mary & D'Andre
Wheelbarrow Race	Isabella & Talos Derek & Mary Ken & D'Andre

Column widths made equal and row heights made equal create a more pleasing table.

QUICK REFERENCE	ADJUSTING COLUMN WIDTHS AND ROW HEIGHTS
Task	**Procedure**
Make manual adjustments	■ The ⁺‖⁺ or ⁼⁼ mouse pointer shape appears whenever the mouse is positioned over a column or row border. You can adjust column widths and row heights by dragging the borders.
Make automatic adjustments	■ Point to a column's right border until the ⁺‖⁺ mouse pointer appears, and then double-click.
Equalize column widths	■ Select the columns you wish to make equal. ■ Choose Table Tools→Layout→Cell Size→Distribute Columns ▦ from the Ribbon.
Equalize row heights	■ Select the rows you wish to make equal. ■ Choose Table Tools→Layout→Cell Size→Distribute Rows ▤ from the Ribbon.

Adjust Column Widths and Row Heights

In this exercise, you will experiment with adjusting column widths and row heights.

Automatically Adjust Column Widths

1. Point to the **column border** between the two columns until your mouse pointer turns into a double-headed arrow.

2. **Double-click** to resize the left column.
   The column to the left of the border you double-clicked automatically resizes to the width of its longest contents.

3. Point to the **right border** of the table until the same double-headed arrow appears, and then **double-click** to adjust the size of the last column.

Manually Adjust Column Widths

4. Follow these steps to manually adjust the width of the left column:

Ⓐ Point to the **column border** between the two columns until your mouse pointer turns into a double-headed arrow.

Ⓑ **Drag** the column border to the right, about halfway through the second column.

The left column widens, but the table does not. The additional space added to the left column was taken from the right column. The right column has become too narrow.

5. Follow these steps to manually widen the right column:

Ⓐ Point to the **right border** of the table until the same double-headed arrow appears.

Ⓑ **Drag** to the right to increase the width of the last column. **Drag** almost to the end of the white area of the slide.

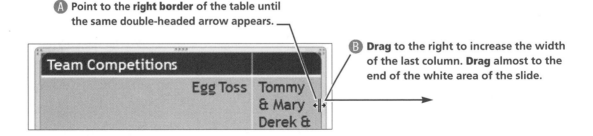

Equalize Column Widths

6. Point to the top of the **left column** until the mouse pointer becomes a thick down arrow, and then **drag** to the right to select both columns.

7. Choose **Table Tools→Layout→Cell Size→ Distribute Columns** from the Ribbon.
The column widths are made equal.

8. **Click** anywhere outside the table to deselect the highlighted cells.

9. **Save** 🖫 your presentation and continue with the next topic.

Adding and Deleting Rows and Columns

Video Lesson   labyrinthelab.com/videos

Adding additional rows to the bottom of a table is as simple as selecting the final cell and tapping the Tab key, but quite often you will want to add rows in the middle or top of the table or to add more columns. This is easily done from the Ribbon. You can also insert multiple rows and columns quickly.

Lost Data

Deleting a row or column also deletes the content. A common mistake users make is to select a row or column and tap Delete. Although that deletes the content inside the cells, it leaves the cells themselves.

QUICK REFERENCE	ADDING AND DELETING ROWS AND COLUMNS
Task	**Procedure**
Insert a row	▪ Click inside any cell you wish to place a row above or below.
	▪ Choose Table Tools→Layout→Rows & Columns→Insert Above or Insert Below.
Insert multiple rows	▪ Select a number of rows equal to the number you wish to insert.
	▪ Choose Table Tools→Layout→Rows & Columns→Insert Above or Insert Below.
Delete a row	▪ Click in any cell in the row you wish to delete, or select multiple rows.
	▪ Choose Table Tools→Layout→Rows & Columns→Delete ▼→Delete Rows.
Insert a column	▪ Click inside any cell you wish to place a column beside.
	▪ Choose Table Tools→Layout→Rows & Columns→Insert Left or Insert Right.
Insert multiple columns	▪ Select a number of columns equal to the number you wish to insert.
	▪ Choose Table Tools→Layout→Rows & Columns→Insert Left or Insert Right.
Delete a column	▪ Click in any cell in the column you wish to delete, or select multiple columns.
	▪ Choose Table Tools→Layout→Rows & Columns→Delete ▼→Delete Columns.

Add and Delete Rows and Columns

In this exercise, you will delete a row and add a column.

Add Multiple Rows

1. **Click** once in the Water Balloon Toss cell.

2. **Press** ⌈Shift⌋, click in the bottom-right cell, and then **release** ⌈Shift⌋.
   The bottom two rows become selected.

3. Choose **Table Tools→Layout→Rows & Columns→Insert Below**.
   Because you selected two rows initially, two additional rows are inserted below your selection. As it happens, you don't need the bottom three rows at all. You will delete them in the next few steps.

Delete Rows

The Piggyback Race was cancelled, so its table row must be deleted.

4. **Click** once in the Piggyback Race cell.

5. **Press and hold** ⌈Shift⌋, **click** in the bottom-right cell, and then **release** ⌈Shift⌋.
   The bottom three rows become selected.

6. Choose **Table Tools→Layout→Rows & Columns→
   Delete ▼→Delete Rows,** as shown in the following figure.
   The Piggyback Race row and additional empty rows are deleted.

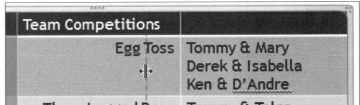

Add Columns

Clip Art will add some visual excitement to the slide. A column is needed to hold the images.

7. **Click** once in the Egg Toss cell.

8. Choose **Table Tools→Layout→Rows & Columns→Insert Left** .
   A new column is inserted to the left of the cell in which you clicked. Some cells in the last column may wrap to four lines.

9. Point to the **column border** to the right of the Egg Toss cell until your mouse pointer becomes a double-headed arrow, and then **drag** the border to the left of the word *Toss*.

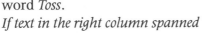

   If text in the right column spanned four lines before, the text now spans three lines. However, the middle column now has text that wraps.

10. Point to the **column border** to the left of the Egg Toss cell until your mouse pointer becomes a double-headed arrow, **drag** the border slightly to the left, and then **release** the mouse button.

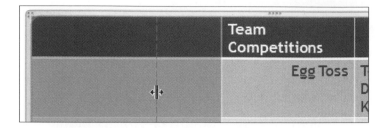

The text in the middle column no longer wraps. If your text still wraps, drag the border a little more to the left. Your slide should resemble the following figure.

11. **Click** anywhere outside the table to deselect the highlighted cells.

12. **Save** 💾 your presentation and continue with the next topic.

Adding Nontext Data to Cells

Video Lesson   labyrinthelab.com/videos

Only text you type at the keyboard can truly reside inside a table cell. If you attempt to insert a picture, chart, or some other object in a cell, it will simply sit on top of the table as an independent object. If you move the table, the overlapping object will not move with the table. If you resize a column or row, it will have no effect on the overlapping object. However, you can make it appear as though the object were inside the table cell by resizing and carefully positioning the object over the cell.

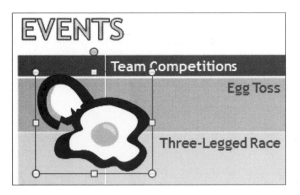

Clip art placed in a table cell actually sits on top of the table as an independent object (left).
Reduced and repositioned artwork appears as if it is truly inside a cell (right).

Add Clip Art over a Cell

In this exercise, you will add clip art and make it appear as though the pictures are in the cells.

1. Choose **Insert→Images→Clip Art** from the Ribbon to open the Clip Art panel.

2. Follow these steps to find clip art for the Egg Toss row:

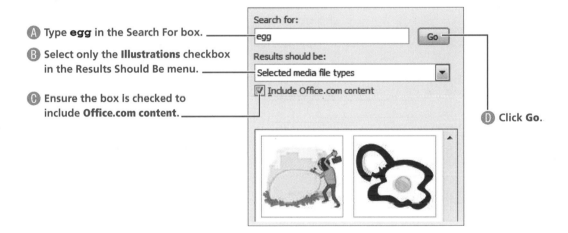

Ⓐ Type **egg** in the Search For box.

Ⓑ Select only the **Illustrations** checkbox in the Results Should Be menu.

Ⓒ Ensure the box is checked to include **Office.com content**.

Ⓓ Click **Go**.

3. **Scroll** through the results until you find a picture you like, and then **click** the picture thumbnail to insert it on the slide.

4. Follow these steps to move and scale the clip art image:

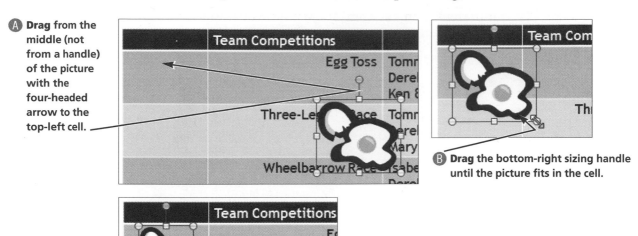

A **Drag** from the middle (not from a handle) of the picture with the four-headed arrow to the top-left cell.

B **Drag** the bottom-right sizing handle until the picture fits in the cell.

C Adjust the size and location of the picture to the center of the cell.

Don't forget that the cursor ([↑], [↓], etc.) keys are useful for adjusting the location of pictures. To make finer adjustments, hold down the [Ctrl] key as you tap a cursor key.

5. Continue to resize and reposition the picture until it fits in the empty cell.

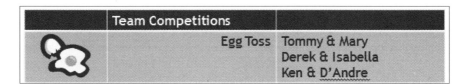

6. Repeat **steps 2–5** with the search term **belt** and position the picture to the left of the Three-Legged Race cell.

7. Repeat **steps 2–5** with the search term **wheelbarrow** and position the picture to the left of the Wheelbarrow Race cell.

8. Repeat **steps 2–5** with the search term **balloon** and position the picture to the left of the Water Balloon Toss cell.
Your table should resemble the following figure.

	Team Competitions	
🥚	Egg Toss	Tommy & Mary Derek & Isabella Ken & D'Andre
👔	Three-Legged Race	Tommy & Talos Derek & Ken Mary & D'Andre
🛠	Wheelbarrow Race	Isabella & Talos Derek & Mary Ken & D'Andre
🎈	Water Balloon Toss	Tommy & Derek Ken & Mary Isabella & D'Andre

9. **Close** the Clip Art panel.

10. **Save** 💾 your presentation and continue with the next topic.

Merging and Splitting Cells

Video Lesson   labyrinthelab.com/videos

Merging cells is the process of selecting multiple cells and combining them into one single larger cell that spans multiple rows or columns. *Splitting* cells is the opposite—cutting a single cell into several smaller cells.

Cells are often merged across the top row of a table to create a single long row that acts as a label for the table. This makes it easier to format the text in the top cell because it can be centered over the entire table rather than just a single cell.

	Team Competitions	
🥚	Egg Toss	Tommy & Mary Derek & Isabella Ken & D'Andre

The top row contains three distinct cells. Although *Team Competitions* is centered in its cell, it is not centered over the entire table.

Team Competitions		
🥚	Egg Toss	Tommy & Mary Derek & Isabella Ken & D'Andre

With the cells across the top row merged, *Team Competitions* can be centered over the entire table.

QUICK REFERENCE	MERGING AND SPLITTING CELLS
Task	**Procedure**
Merge cells	▪ Select the cells you wish to merge. ▪ Choose Table Tools→Layout→Merge→Merge Cells from the Ribbon.
Split cells	▪ Click in the single cell you wish to split. ▪ Choose Table Tools→Layout→Merge→Split Cells from the Ribbon. ▪ Enter the number of columns and rows you wish to split the cell into, and then click OK.

Merge Cells

In this exercise, you will merge cells and finalize the cell alignment.

1. **Click** once in the top-left empty cell.

2. **Press** ⟨Shift⟩, **click** once in the top-right empty cell, and then **release** ⟨Shift⟩.
   All cells in the top row are selected.

3. Choose **Table Tools→Layout→Merge→Merge Cells** ⊞ from the Ribbon.
   The cells in the top row are merged into a single long cell. The text in this cell would look better if it were centered over the table.

4. Choose **Table Tools→Layout→Alignment→Center** from the Ribbon.

5. Point to the **Egg Toss** cell and then drag down to the **Water Balloon Toss** cell.
   Four cells down the middle column become selected.

6. Choose **Table Tools→Layout→Alignment→Center** from the Ribbon.
   The text becomes centered in its cells.

7. **Click** anywhere outside the table to deselect the highlighted cells.

8. **Save** 💾 your presentation and continue with the next topic.

7.2 Customizing Tables

Video Lesson   labyrinthelab.com/videos

The contextual Design and Layout tabs on the Ribbon provide many commands with which to customize the appearance of tables and cells. You can apply borders and shading to cells in the table, change the alignment of text, add rows or columns, apply shadows, bevels, and other visual effects, and make many other adjustments.

Applying Table Styles

You can use table styles to quickly and easily apply colors, shading, background patterns, bevels, and other special effects to tables and table cells. PowerPoint offers professionally created color schemes to complement your document theme, taking much of the guesswork out of applying color.

You can choose from several preset color schemes, which are organized in Light, Medium, Dark, and Best Match for Document categories. Additionally, table styles can be customized by designating certain rows or columns to receive a slightly different color. For example, the top row of a table may be a different color than the rest of the cells to emphasize the table's title. You can also add background colors, background pictures, gradients, textures, bevels, and shadows to tables. The following figures compare a simple table before and after table styles were applied.

	Sack Race	100-Yard Dash	Archery
1st place	Tommy	Mary	Derek
2nd place	Isabella	Ken	Jenna
3rd place	Nicole	Amy	Brian

Table with no formatting applied

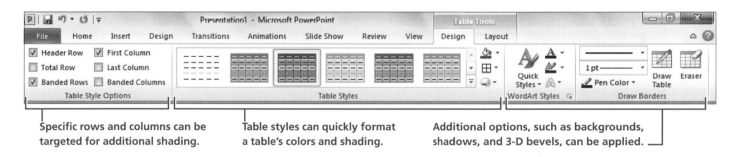

	Sack Race	100-Yard Dash	Archery
1st place	Tommy	Mary	Derek
2nd place	Isabella	Ken	Jenna
3rd place	Nicole	Amy	Brian

The same table with a table style and options applied

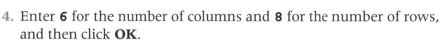

Specific rows and columns can be targeted for additional shading. | Table styles can quickly format a table's colors and shading. | Additional options, such as backgrounds, shadows, and 3-D bevels, can be applied.

DEVELOP YOUR SKILLS 7.2.1

Apply Table Styles

In this exercise, you will create a new table and apply a table style to it.

Create the Table

1. If necessary, select the **Events** slide, and then choose **Home→Slides→New Slide** from the Ribbon.

2. Type **Totals** as the slide title.

3. Click the **Insert Table** icon in the center of the slide, as shown at right.
   The Insert Table dialog box appears.

4. Enter **6** for the number of columns and **8** for the number of rows, and then click **OK**.
   PowerPoint creates a table with six columns and eight rows on the slide. The table is already formatted with the color scheme of the document theme.

5. Using the $\boxed{\text{Tab}}$ key to navigate the cells, fill in the following table data:

	Egg Toss	Three-Legged Race	Wheelbarrow Race	Water Balloon Toss	Total
Tommy	5	5	0	5	15
Talos	0	5	5	0	10
Ken	1	3	1	3	8
Mary	5	1	3	3	12
D'Andre	1	1	1	1	4
Isabella	3	0	5	1	9
Derek	3	3	3	5	14

Some of the contest names wrap in an undesirable way. A smaller font and adjusted column widths will fix that.

6. Point to the border of the table until your mouse pointer becomes a four-headed arrow, and then **click** once to select the entire table.
The change on the screen is very subtle. The border still displays around the table, but the insertion point in the cell disappears, indicating that the entire table has been selected.

7. Choose **Home→Font→Font Size ▼→16** from the Ribbon.
The font is reduced for the entire table, but the contest names still wrap. You will adjust the column widths to fix them.

8. Point to the right border of the Water Balloon Toss column until your mouse pointer becomes a double-headed arrow, and then **drag** slightly to the right to manually fit the column.
You may have to drag, release the mouse button, drag, and release the mouse button several times to get it just right. Your table should resemble the following figure.

9. Continue to resize the other columns until your table resembles the following figure.

Egg Toss	Three-Legged Race	Wheelbarrow Race	Water Balloon Toss	Total

Apply a Table Style

10. **Click** once in any cell, and then choose **Table Tools→Design→Table Styles→More** from the Ribbon.
The Table Styles gallery opens but covers your table.

11. Point to any of the table styles in the **Table Styles** gallery to see a Live Preview of the style on your slide.
Your table changes as you point to different styles, but your table is hidden behind the Table Styles gallery.

12. **Tap** $\boxed{\text{Esc}}$ to close the Table Styles gallery without applying a style.

13. Follow these steps to apply a table style:

Ⓐ Point to any **Table Styles** thumbnail to preview the style on your slide.

Ⓑ **Click** the scroll-down button to load the next row of table styles in the Ribbon.

Ⓒ Point to several more table styles to preview them on your slide.

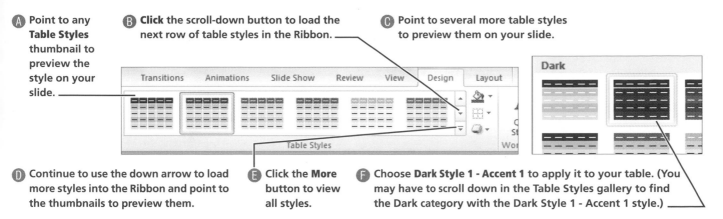

Ⓓ Continue to use the down arrow to load more styles into the Ribbon and point to the thumbnails to preview them.

Ⓔ **Click** the **More** button to view all styles.

Ⓕ Choose **Dark Style 1 - Accent 1** to apply it to your table. (You may have to scroll down in the Table Styles gallery to find the Dark category with the Dark Style 1 - Accent 1 style.)

PowerPoint applies your selection to the entire table.

14. Save 💾 your presentation and continue with the next topic.

Applying Table Style Options

Video Lesson labyrinthelab.com/videos

You are not stuck with the basic formatting applied by a table style. You can modify the table after applying a style to include additional shading or add backgrounds to the table cells.

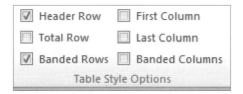

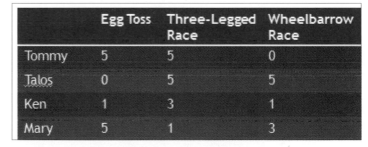

Use the Table Style Options command group to apply additional shading to specific rows or columns. The Header Row option applied a different color to the top row while the Banded Rows option applied different colors to alternating rows.

QUICK REFERENCE	APPLYING TABLE STYLE OPTIONS
Option	**Where Additional Shading Is Applied**
Header Row	Top row
Total Row	Bottom row
Banded Rows	Row colors alternate, with odd rows one shade and even rows a different shade
First Column	Left column
Last Column	Right column
Banded Columns	Column colors alternate, with odd columns one shade and even columns a different shade

Apply Table Style Options

In this exercise, you will apply table style options to your table.

Align Cell Contents

1. Point to the left of the top row until your mouse pointer becomes a thick right arrow, and then **click** to select the entire top row.

2. Choose **Table Tools→Layout→Alignment→Center** from the Ribbon.
   The text in the top row becomes center-aligned.

3. Point to the first cell in the second row, with the text Tommy.

4. **Drag down** to the last cell in the first column to select the seven cells with employee names.

5. Choose **Table Tools→Layout→Alignment→Align Text Right** from the Ribbon.
   The employee names are right-aligned in their cells.

6. Select all the cells in the body of the table that contain numbers.

7. Choose **Table Tools→Layout→Alignment→Center** ☰ from the Ribbon.
   Your table should now resemble the following figure (yours may display white column lines if the table is selected).

	Egg Toss	Three-Legged Race	Wheelbarrow Race	Water Balloon Toss	Total
Tommy	5	5	0	5	15
Talos	0	5	5	0	10
Ken	1	3	1	3	8
Mary	5	1	3	3	12
D'Andre	1	1	1	1	4
Isabella	3	0	5	1	9
Derek	3	3	3	5	14

Apply Custom Shading

8. Select the **Table Tools→Design→Table Style Options→Last Column** checkbox.
   The Totals column receives darker shading.

9. Select the **seven cells** in the **first column** containing employee names.

 In the next step, you will create a visual effect called a gradient fill for the table.

10. Follow these steps to apply a gradient background to the cells:

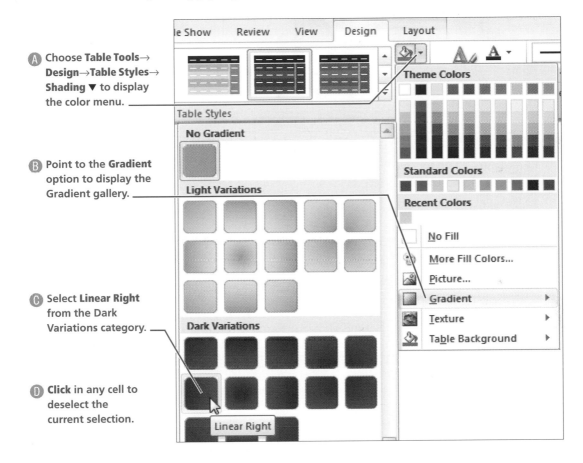

Ⓐ Choose **Table Tools→ Design→Table Styles→ Shading ▼** to display the color menu.

Ⓑ Point to the **Gradient** option to display the Gradient gallery.

Ⓒ Select **Linear Right** from the Dark Variations category.

Ⓓ **Click** in any cell to deselect the current selection.

The employee name cells receive a gradient background.

Apply Custom Background Colors

You will color the Total cells to indicate first place, second place, and third place.

11. **Click** once inside Tommy's Total cell, the last cell in the second row.

12. Follow these steps to color Tommy's Total cell blue:

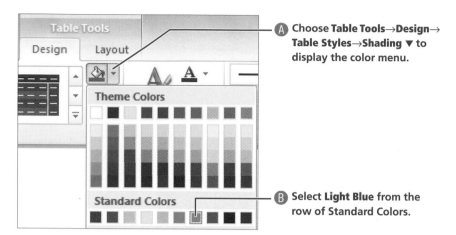

Ⓐ Choose **Table Tools→Design→ Table Styles→Shading ▼** to display the color menu.

Ⓑ Select **Light Blue** from the row of Standard Colors.

13. **Click** inside Derek's Total cell, with a score of 14.

14. Choose **Table Tools→Design→Table Styles→Shading ▼→ Standard Colors→Red**.

15. **Click** inside Mary's Total cell, with a score of 12, and apply a **background color** of orange.

Apply 3-D Bevels

16. Point to the table border until your mouse pointer becomes a four-headed arrow, and then **click** to select the entire table.

17. Follow these steps to apply a 3-D bevel to the table cells:

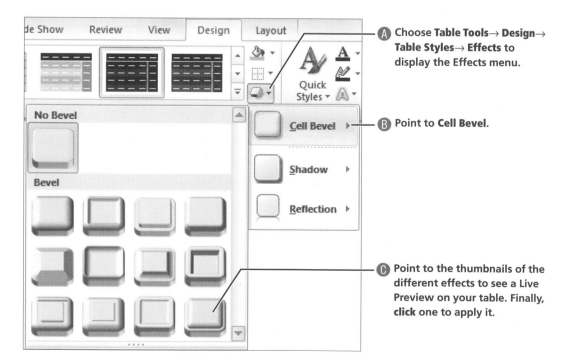

Ⓐ Choose **Table Tools→ Design→ Table Styles→ Effects** to display the Effects menu.

Ⓑ Point to **Cell Bevel**.

Ⓒ Point to the thumbnails of the different effects to see a Live Preview on your table. Finally, **click** one to apply it.

The effect is applied to all cells. However, it is barely noticeable along the top row because the row is black and the bevel shading cannot be seen.

18. Select all cells in the **top row**.

19. Choose **Table Tools→Design→Table Styles→Shading ▾→Theme Colors→Pink Text 2** from the Ribbon.
    The 3-D bevel on the top row is now visible. Your table should resemble the following figure.

	Egg Toss	Three-Legged Race	Wheelbarrow Race	Water Balloon Toss	Total
Tommy	5	5	0	5	15
Talos	0	5	5	0	10
Ken	1	3	1	3	8
Mary	5	1	3	3	12
D'Andre	1	1	1	1	4
Isabella	3	0	5	1	9
Derek	3	3	3	5	14

20. **Save** 🔲 your presentation and continue with the next topic.

Aligning a Table

Video Lesson   labyrinthelab.com/videos

After the cell formatting is complete, a good final step is to position the table exactly where you want on the slide. Although you can drag the table to any location and eyeball it, you will achieve more exact results with the Align option. Using the Align option lets you center the table perfectly in the middle of the slide, or align the table to any edge of the slide.

QUICK REFERENCE	ALIGNING A TABLE
Task	**Procedure**
Align a table to a specific location within a slide	■ Click in any cell so the table displays its border. ■ Choose the Table Tools→Layout→Arrange→ ⊞ Align ▾ menu from the Ribbon. ■ Select Align Left, Align Center, or Align Right to shift the table horizontally. ■ Select Align Top, Align Middle, or Align Bottom to shift the table vertically.

Align a Table to a Slide

In this exercise, you will position the table in the exact vertical center of the slide.

1. **Click** inside any table cell on the Totals slide.

2. Choose **Table Tools**→**Layout**→**Arrange**→ 📊 Align ▾ →**Align Middle** from the Ribbon.
   The table becomes centered vertically.

3. Choose **Table Tools**→**Layout**→**Arrange**→ 📊 Align ▾ →**Align Center** from the Ribbon.
   The table becomes cantered horizontally, but because the document theme includes a stripe of color along the right edge of the slide, the table looks unbalanced if centered horizontally.

4. Choose **Quick Access Toolbar**→**Undo** 🔄 .
   The table shifts back to its original horizontal position, which appears centered in the white area of the slide.

5. **Save** 💾 your presentation.

7.3 Concepts Review

Concepts Review	labyrinthelab.com/pp10

To check your knowledge of the key concepts introduced in this lesson, complete the Concepts Review quiz by going to the URL listed above. If your classroom is using Labyrinth eLab, you may complete the Concepts Review quiz from within your eLab course.

Reinforce Your Skills

Insert a Table

In this exercise, you will insert a table and add text.

Insert a Table

1. **Start** PowerPoint, **maximize** the program window, and **open** the rs-Featured Homes presentation from the Lesson 07 folder.

2. Choose **Home→Slides→New Slide** to insert a new slide after the title slide, and then type **This Month** as the title.

3. Click the **Insert Table** icon on the slide and insert a table with three columns and ten rows.

4. In the top-left cell, type **March 2010 Featured Properties**.

5. Fill in the remaining rows as in the following table:

Price	Bedrooms	Bathrooms
$750,000	3	3.5
$600,000	4	3.5
$500,000	3	3
$1,600,000	5	4.5
$380,000	3	2.5
$1,300,000	4	3
$2,100,000	6	5
$450,000	4	3

6. **Save** your presentation and continue with the next exercise.

Work with Rows and Columns

In this exercise, you will add and delete rows and columns, merge cells, adjust cell widths, and align the table to the slide.

Before You Begin: You must have completed Reinforce Your Skills 7.1, and the rs-Featured Homes presentation should be open.

Delete a Row

1. **Click** in the $500,000 cell.

2. Choose **Table Tools→Layout→Rows & Columns→Delete ▾→Delete Rows**.

Add Columns

3. Point to the **Bedrooms** cell and drag across to the Bathrooms cell so both cells are selected.
By selecting two cells, you have also selected two columns.

4. Choose **Table Tools→Layout→Rows & Columns→Insert Left**.
Because two columns were selected, two columns were inserted.

5. Starting with the second row, **type** the following in the new columns:

Sq. Ft.	Acreage
4000	4
3400	.32
5600	2
2700	.25
4200	.6
6100	.6
2900	.28

Merge Cells

6. Select all cells across the **top row**.

7. Choose **Table Tools→Layout→Merge→Merge Cells** from the Ribbon.

Resize Columns

8. Point to the right of the Price column until the mouse pointer becomes a double-headed arrow, and then **double-click** to automatically adjust the width of the Price column.

9. Repeat **step 8** for the other four columns to automatically adjust their widths.

Center the Table

10. Choose **Table Tools→Layout→Arrange→Align→Align Center** to horizontally center the table on the slide.

11. Choose **Table Tools→Layout→Arrange→Align→Align Middle** to vertically center the table on the slide.

12. **Save** your presentation and continue with the next exercise.

Format the Table

In this exercise, you will apply table styles and configure style options.

Before You Begin: *You must have completed Reinforce Your Skills 7.2, and the rs-Featured Homes presentation should be open.*

1. If necessary, **click** inside any table cell so the table border displays.

2. Choose **Table Tools→Design→Table Styles→More** ▼ **→Best Match** for **Document→Themed Style 1 Accent 5** from the Ribbon.

3. Select the checkbox for the **Table Tools→Design→Table Style Options→First Column** setting so the Price column receives additional formatting.

4. **Click** once in the top merged cell, and then choose **Table Tools→Layout→Alignment→ Center** from the Ribbon to center the text in its cell.

5. Select the **eight cells** in the Price column and choose **Table Tools→Layout→ Alignment→Align Text Right** from the Ribbon to right-align the text in their cells.

6. Select the remaining cells in the **last four columns** and center the text in the cells.

7. Choose **Table Tools→Design→Table Styles→Effects→Shadow→Perspective→Perspective Diagonal Upper Left** from the Ribbon to add a 3-D shadow to the table.

8. **Save** and **close** your presentation.

Apply Your Skills

Insert and Modify a Table

In this exercise, you will insert a table and format cells.

1. **Open** the as-Tropical Getaways presentation from the Lesson 07 folder and select the **Travel Now and Save**! slide.

2. Insert a table with four columns and four rows and **type** the following text:

FEATURED PACKAGES			
	Location	Total Days	Price
Package 1	Oahu	5	$429
Package 2	Tahiti	7	$1,299

3. Insert a new **row** at the bottom named `Package 3` that offers `Fiji` for `5` days for `$1,000`.

4. Add a new **column** on the right side, label it `Airfare`, and type `included` for all three packages.

5. Merge the **top five cells** and center the text in the large cell. Your table should resemble the following figure.

Featured Packages				
	Location	Total Days	Price	Airfare
Package 1	Oahu	5	$429	included
Package 2	Tahiti	7	$1,299	included
Package 3	Fiji	5	$1,000	included

6. **Save** your presentation and continue with the next exercise.

Apply Table Styles

In this exercise, you will apply and configure table styles.

Before You Begin: You must have completed Apply Your Skills 7.1, the as-Tropical Getaways presentation should be open, and the Travel Now and Save! slide should be displayed.

1. Apply the **Themed Style 2 Accent 2** style to the table on the Travel Now and Save! slide.

2. Make all text in the second row **bold**.

3. Select all cells except the top row and **center-align** the text horizontally in their cells.

4. Automatically adjust the **width** of each column so that it's no wider than necessary to contain the content.

5. **Center** the table in the exact middle of the slide by using PowerPoint's alignment tools.

6. Apply a **shadow effect** to the table.

Pause as you point to each thumbnail in the Shadow menu to display a pop-up ToolTip with the name of the shadow.

7. Click in the top row (the large merged cell) and apply **Orange Accent 6** (the last color in the Themed Colors row) to that row.

8. **Save** your presentation and continue with the next exercise.

Critical Thinking & Work-Readiness Skills

In the course of working through the following Microsoft Office-based Critical Thinking exercises, you will also be utilizing various work-readiness skills, some of which are listed next to each exercise. Go to labyrinthelab.com/ workreadiness to learn more about the work-readiness skills.

7.1 Add a Table

WORK-READINESS SKILLS APPLIED

- Serving clients/ customers
- Thinking creatively
- Seeing things in the mind's eye

In preparation for a Green Clean sales presentation, you are asked to highlight some of the eco-friendly cleaning products used by your company. Create a new presentation consisting of exactly two slides and any theme you like. Create an appropriate title slide. On the second slide, insert a 4 row 3 column table. Size and position the table so it fills the slide as much as possible while maintaining visibility of the slide title. Fill in the top row of cells with appropriate column headings where the first column will feature product images, the second column product names, and the third column product prices. Search for clip art to position within the first column and invent catchy product names and appropriate prices to complete the remaining cells. Size the columns appropriately and save your presentation to your Lesson 07 folder as **ct-Products**.

7.2 Format a Table

WORK-READINESS SKILLS APPLIED

- Thinking creatively
- Seeing things in the mind's eye
- Interpreting and communicating information

Start with the ct-Products presentation you created in the previous exercise and save a copy of it with the name **ct-Enhanced Table** to your Lesson 07 folder. Experiment with table styles and effects to add visual interest. Adjust the row heights and column widths as necessary. Apply a picture style to the images. Save your changes.

7.3 Expand a Table

WORK-READINESS SKILLS APPLIED

- Thinking creatively
- Seeing things in the mind's eye
- Interpreting and communicating information

Open the ct-Enhanced Table presentation you created in the previous exercise and save it to your Lesson 07 folder with the new name **ct-Uses**. Insert a new row at the top of the table and merge it so it becomes one wide cell. Use this merged cell to title your table and format it appropriately. Add a new column to the left of the prices column and add an appropriate column heading and cell text to describe the uses for each product. Save your changes.

Customizing Themes and Slide Masters

LEARNING OBJECTIVES

After studying this lesson, you will be able to:

- Customize a document theme
- Save and reuse a customized document theme
- Edit slide masters
- Insert and format action buttons

In this lesson, you will focus on customizing themes in PowerPoint 2010. You will learn how to customize color schemes and backgrounds, and then save a document theme as your own so you can reuse it as often as you like. In addition, you will edit slide masters to affect multiple slides at once. Finally, you will learn how to incorporate action buttons so you can add functionality to your slide show.

Saving Time with Themes

Green Clean is planning to expand. In their quest to secure more funding to help the new branches flourish, Derek Navarro (Vice President of Operations) needs to create multiple presentations to deliver to various boards, committees, and conferences. He chooses one of his favorite presentations to customize and save as a Green Clean Theme to help him establish a standard corporate image. Although he thought it would be a chore, Derek finds that customizing the document theme is easy. He changes the color scheme of the original design to match the colors most used by Green Clean in their advertisements.

Derek plans to display his presentation at a kiosk during the upcoming EnviroProducts Trade Show. To make navigating through the slide show easy for the viewers, he adds attractive action buttons on each page. Derek discovers that he can even add the action buttons to the slide master, saving himself tedious work.

These action buttons on a slide master appear automatically on each new slide of the presentation.

8.1 Customizing Document Themes

Video Lesson labyrinthelab.com/videos

PowerPoint 2010 comes with forty built-in document themes that contain predesigned formats and color schemes you can apply to a presentation. Although this makes it easy to format a presentation with a consistent set of colors, fonts, and backgrounds, it may not always meet your needs. For example, you may like the slide background and fonts used in a certain document theme, but the colors may not match your company's official advertising colors used in the logo or other promotional materials. With PowerPoint's customization options, you can create custom color schemes or font schemes and apply them to any existing document theme. You can also use your custom colors, fonts, backgrounds, and effects to create an entirely new document theme.

Knowing What You Can Customize

There are several ways to customize any document theme, including:

- Color scheme
- Fonts
- Effects such as shadows and bevels
- Slide background

Customizations That Work Best

The best presentation document theme designs are simple, include a minimal number of fonts and background elements, make good use of white space, and have a pleasant color scheme. Keeping the design simple ensures that the purpose of the slide is not lost.

Customizing the Color Scheme

A color scheme is composed of twelve individual colors for text, backgrounds, hyperlinks, and various accents used for things such as bullets and slide titles. PowerPoint comes with forty-one built-in color schemes—one for each of the forty document themes and one grayscale color scheme. You can customize an existing color scheme by changing one color or all of the colors. You can base a new color scheme on any of the built-in color schemes; however, you cannot edit or delete the built-in color schemes themselves. When you create and save a new color scheme, PowerPoint automatically applies it to all the slides in the current presentation. The new color scheme is also added to available themes on the Ribbon. After you create a custom color scheme, you can apply it to one slide or the entire presentation. You can also edit and delete custom color schemes.

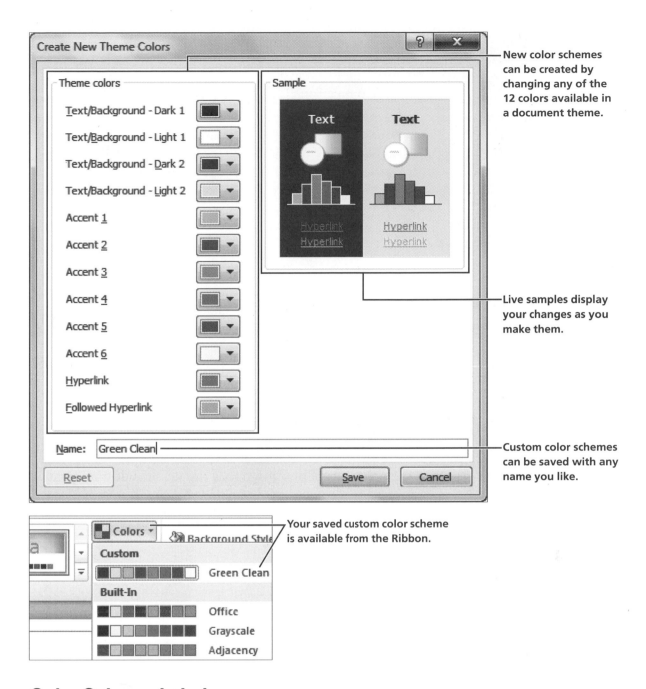

New color schemes can be created by changing any of the 12 colors available in a document theme.

Live samples display your changes as you make them.

Custom color schemes can be saved with any name you like.

Your saved custom color scheme is available from the Ribbon.

Color Scheme Labels

PowerPoint has 12 fixed labels for all color scheme settings, as shown in the Theme Colors section in the preceding figure. Unfortunately, the colors are not labeled in such a way that makes sense. There is no *slide title* label or *bulleted text* label. You need to study the slide and then determine which colors in the dialog box affect the various objects on the slide. For example, some document themes use the Accent 4 color to color the slide title text while another document theme may use the Accent 6 color.

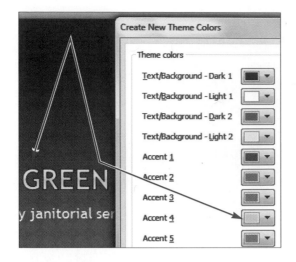

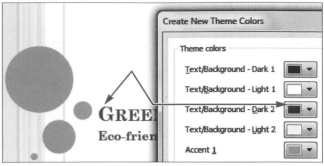

The Opulent theme gets its slide title color from the Accent 4 setting, whereas the Oriel theme gets its slide title color from the Text/Background – Dark 2 setting.

Task	Procedure
Create a new custom color scheme	■ Choose Design→Themes→Colors→Create New Theme Colors from the Ribbon. ■ Choose a new color for any of the 12 theme colors. ■ Type a name for your custom color scheme in the Name box and then click Save. ■ The new color scheme is immediately applied to all slides in the presentation.
Apply a custom color scheme	■ Choose Design→Themes→Colors from the Ribbon. ■ Click the custom color scheme to apply it to all slides. *or* ■ Right-click the custom color scheme and choose Apply to Selected Slides to apply the color scheme to selected slides only.
Edit a custom color scheme	■ Choose Design→Themes→Colors from the Ribbon. ■ Right-click the custom color scheme you wish to edit and choose Edit from the pop-up menu. ■ Change the colors as desired and then click Save.
Delete a custom color scheme	■ Choose Design→Themes→Colors from the Ribbon. ■ Right-click the custom color scheme you wish to edit and choose Delete from the context menu to remove the scheme from the Ribbon. ■ If the custom color scheme was used on any slides, the slides will not be affected. The custom color scheme will simply no longer be available to apply to additional slides.

Create and Apply Custom Colors

In this exercise, you will create and apply a custom color scheme.

Apply a Built-in Color Scheme

1. **Start** PowerPoint and **maximize** the program window.

2. **Open** the Green Clean Custom presentation from the Lesson 08 folder.
   The presentation has the Civic theme applied, which includes colors a little duller than we want to use.

3. Follow these steps to apply a built-in color scheme:

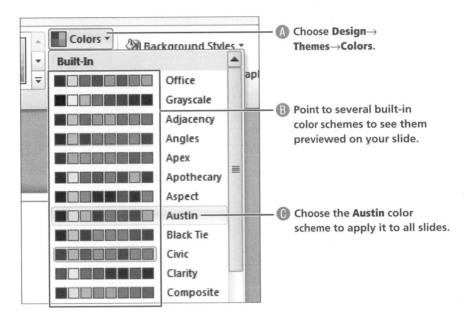

A Choose **Design→ Themes→Colors.**

B Point to several built-in color schemes to see them previewed on your slide.

C Choose the **Austin** color scheme to apply it to all slides.

The color scheme on all slides has been changed from the drab grays of the Civic theme to the green and orange of the Austin theme.

Create a Custom Color Scheme

The Austin color scheme is close, but has too much orange for Green Clean. You will alter the color scheme in the next steps.

4. Choose **Design→Themes→** [Colors ▾] **→ Create New Theme Colors** from the Ribbon.
   The Create New Theme Colors dialog box opens.

5. Follow these steps to create a custom color scheme:

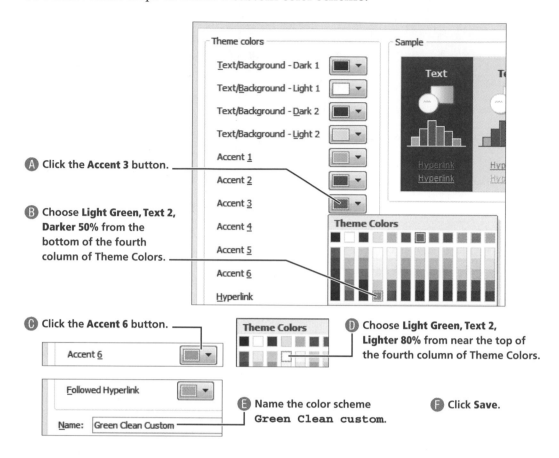

Ⓐ Click the **Accent 3** button.

Ⓑ Choose **Light Green, Text 2, Darker 50%** from the bottom of the fourth column of Theme Colors.

Ⓒ Click the **Accent 6** button.

Ⓓ Choose **Light Green, Text 2, Lighter 80%** from near the top of the fourth column of Theme Colors.

Ⓔ Name the color scheme **Green Clean custom**.

Ⓕ Click **Save**.

The custom color scheme is applied to all slides, and you see the new colors on the current slide.

6. **Save** 💾 your presentation.

Changing a Slide Background

Video Lesson   labyrinthelab.com/videos

You can change the background for one slide or the entire presentation. You can choose from preset backgrounds tailored to your document theme, or you can create your own custom background that overrides the document theme. You might want to change the color, use an image, or add a textured look such as wood, marble, or fabric. You can also add color effects to vary the pattern and intensity of the color. For example, you can use a Gradient effect, which fades from dark to light across a slide, or use a variety of Texture effects. You can experiment with custom backgrounds without fear of ruining your presentation because PowerPoint offers a Reset Slide Background command that resets the slide's background to the previous background.

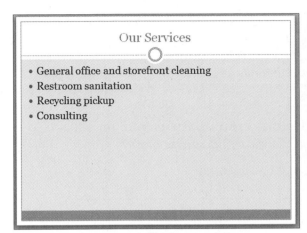 

The same slide with a gradient background (left) and a textured marble background (right).

Using a Preset Background

Each document theme comes with 12 preset, coordinated backgrounds. You can choose one of these preset backgrounds to modify the look of your presentation without worrying whether the background will clash with the rest of the design. Because the backgrounds are part of the document theme, they are designed to match. When you select a preset background, PowerPoint applies it to all slides in the presentation. Choosing a new document theme will change the background on all slides.

The 12 preset backgrounds match the current document theme.

The background applied to the selected slide is highlighted.

The Format Background command allows you to customize the background and override the document theme presets.

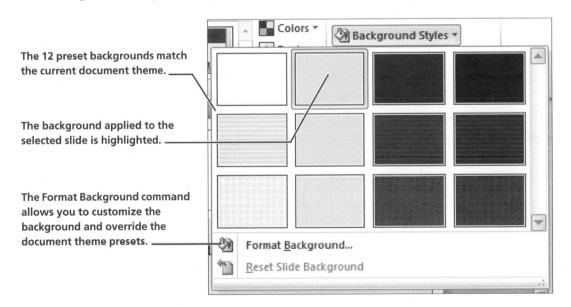

Apply a Preset Background

In this exercise, you will use the preset backgrounds included with the document theme.

1. Display the second slide, **Our Services**.

2. Choose **Design→Background→Background Styles** from the Ribbon.
   PowerPoint displays the 12 background styles for the current theme.

3. Follow these steps to apply a preset background:

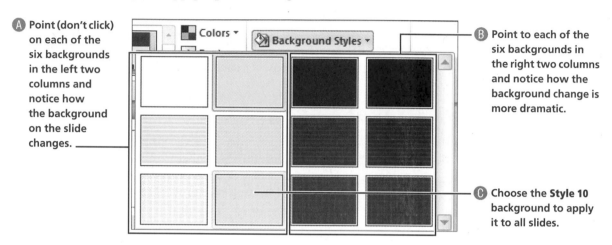

A Point (don't click) on each of the six backgrounds in the left two columns and notice how the background on the slide changes.

B Point to each of the six backgrounds in the right two columns and notice how the background change is more dramatic.

C Choose the **Style 10** background to apply it to all slides.

4. Choose **Design→Background→Background Styles** from the Ribbon.
   The Reset Slide Background command is not available because the current background is part of the document theme.

5. **Click** anywhere outside the drop-down menu to close it without applying any changes.

6. Choose **Design→Themes→More** ⏷→**Equity** to apply the Equity document theme.
   PowerPoint applies the Equity theme, and the slide backgrounds are reset to the Equity theme default.

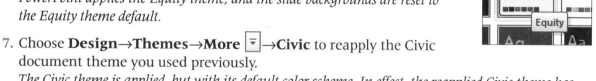

7. Choose **Design→Themes→More** ⏷→**Civic** to reapply the Civic document theme you used previously.
   The Civic theme is applied, but with its default color scheme. In effect, the reapplied Civic theme has replaced the manual customization you created earlier.

8. Choose **Design→Themes→Colors→Green Clean** custom from the Ribbon.
   PowerPoint applies your new custom color scheme.

9. **Save** 🖫 your presentation.

Creating a Gradient Fill

Video Lesson   labyrinthelab.com/videos

You can customize a background with a single solid color or with a *gradient fill*. A gradient fill consists of several colors that blend into one another. PowerPoint includes several preset gradients, but you can also create your own.

A Radial gradient (left) and a Path gradient (right)

How Gradients Are Defined

Gradients in PowerPoint backgrounds may contain as few as two and as many as ten different *stops*. A stop defines a color, a position, a brightness value, and a transparency. The color setting defines the color used. That's obvious. The position defines where the gradient occurs. The brightness defines how light or dark the color is. Increasing brightness adds white to lighten the color while decreasing the brightness adds black to darken the color. The transparency defines whether a color is fading out. A transparency of 0% means the color is not transparent at all and is at full color. A transparency of 100% means the color is invisible. A transparency of 50% means the color is very faded. Additional gradient settings include the shape of gradient (in what direction the colors blend, such as from the center out or diagonally) and the direction of the gradient, which determines whether the colors blend from the top down, left to right, and so on.

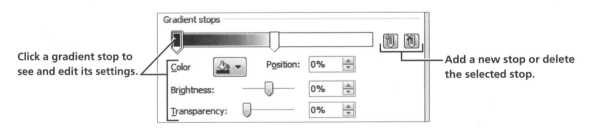

Click a gradient stop to see and edit its settings.

Add a new stop or delete the selected stop.

Setting Stop Positions

There are many ways to configure a custom gradient, and without doubt, setting the stop position is the most confusing. One simple method is to always set the first stop to 0% and then set subsequent stop positions based on where the colors should stop blending. For example, consider a simple two-color gradient that blends from top to bottom. The first color is set to a position of 0%. The second color is set to a position of 50%. The gradient blend would occur entirely in the top half of the slide (from 0%–50%). At 50%, the second color would be completely displayed with no more blend.

Stop 1 is set to black with a stop position of 0% so that the gradient blend begins immediately.

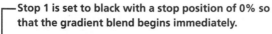
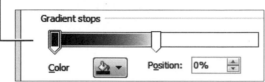

Stop 2 is set to light gray with a stop position of 50% so that the blend stops and only the light gray remains.

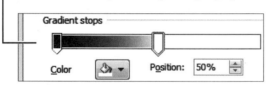

The gradient occurs from 0% to 50%. At 50%, the gradient stops and the slide is pure light gray.

Stop 1 is set to black with a stop position of 25% so that the top quarter of the slide is solid black. The gradient blend starts at 25%.

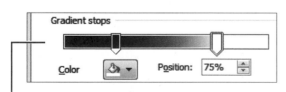

Stop 2 is set to light gray with a stop position of 75% so that the gradient blend stops ³/₄ of the way down the slide.

From 0%–25% the slide is pure black. From 25%–75% there is a gradient blend. At 75%, the gradient stops and the slide is pure light gray.

Task	Procedure
Apply a preset gradient as a custom background	■ Choose Design→Background→Background Styles→Format Background from the Ribbon. ■ Choose the Gradient Fill option. ■ Choose a gradient color scheme from the Preset Colors menu. ■ Choose a gradient type from the Type menu. ■ Choose a direction for the gradient blend from the Direction menu. ■ Customize the direction by changing the angle in the Angle box. ■ Click Close to apply the gradient to the selected slide(s). *or* ■ Click Apply to All to apply the gradient to all slides.
Apply a custom gradient as a custom background	■ Choose Design→Background→Background Styles→Format Background from the Ribbon. ■ Choose the Gradient Fill option. ■ Click Add Gradient Stop 📑 or Remove Gradient Stop 📑 . ■ Click the left-most step from the Gradient Stops bar and set a position, color, brightness, and transparency. ■ Choose the remaining stops from the Gradient Stops menu and set positions, colors, brightness, and transparencies as desired. ■ Click Close to apply the gradient to the selected slide(s). *or* ■ Click Apply to All to apply the gradient to all slides.

Apply Gradient Backgrounds

In this exercise, you will apply a preset gradient and create a custom gradient background.

Apply a Preset Gradient

1. If necessary, select the second slide, **Our Services**.

2. Choose **Design→Background→Background Styles→Format Background** from the Ribbon and follow these steps to apply a preset gradient:

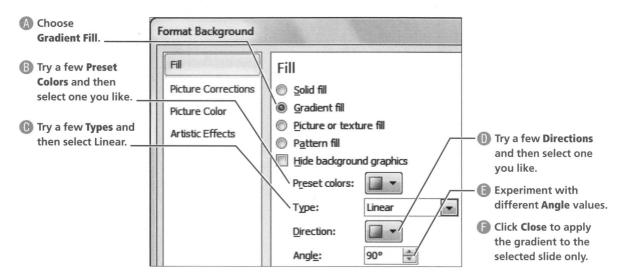

Ⓐ Choose **Gradient Fill.**

Ⓑ Try a few **Preset Colors** and then select one you like.

Ⓒ Try a few **Types** and then select Linear.

Ⓓ Try a few **Directions** and then select one you like.

Ⓔ Experiment with different **Angle** values.

Ⓕ Click **Close** to apply the gradient to the selected slide only.

Reset a Slide Background

3. Choose **Design→Background→Background Styles→Reset Slide Background** from the Ribbon.
The slide background is reset to the previous background.

Create a Custom Gradient

Now you will create a simple custom gradient fill with just two stops.

4. Choose **Design→Background→Background Styles→Format Background** from the Ribbon and follow these steps to create exactly two stops:

Ⓐ If there are more than two stops, **click** any stop to select it.

Ⓑ Click **Remove Gradient Stop** to remove the stop.

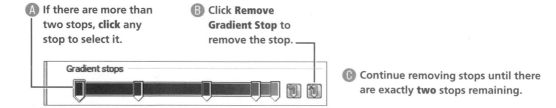

Ⓒ Continue removing stops until there are exactly **two** stops remaining.

5. Follow these steps to create a custom gradient:

Ⓐ Drag the left-most stop until its position is 25%.

Ⓑ Select **Light Green, Background 2, Darker 50%** from the bottom of the third column of the color menu.

Ⓒ Ensure Brightness is set to **–50%** and Transparency is set to **0%**.

Ⓓ **Click** to select the second stop.

Ⓔ Type **75** in the Position box to set its position to 75%.

Ⓕ Select **Green, Accent 1, Lighter 80%** from the top of the fifth column of the color menu.

Ⓖ Ensure Brightness is set to **80%** and Transparency is set to **0%**.

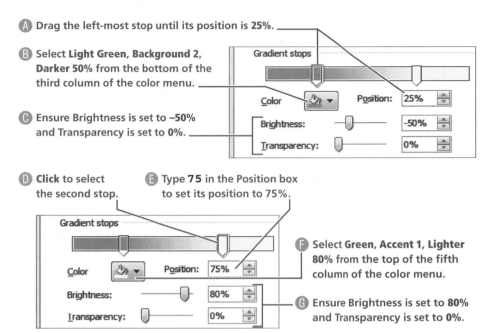

PowerPoint displays the effects of the new stop settings. You could add still more stops, but instead let's see how the other gradient settings can work with just two stops.

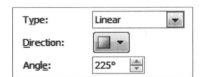

6. Experiment with the Type, Direction, and Angle settings shown at right until you are satisfied with the custom gradient.

7. Click **Apply to All** to apply the gradient to all slides and then click **Close**.

8. **Save** 🖫 your presentation.

Using Pictures or Textures for Backgrounds

Video Lesson   labyrinthelab.com/videos

PowerPoint offers 24 textures you can use as slide backgrounds, including wood, marble, and paper textures. You can also use clip art images or image files from your computer, such as a photo from a digital camera, as a slide background.

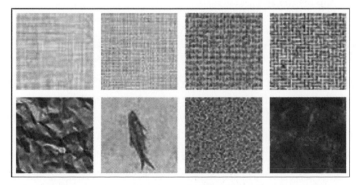

A few of the 24 textures provided with PowerPoint

Picture and Texture Background Settings

When you select a texture or insert a picture to use as a background, there are several settings you can configure to control how the background looks. The main Tile Picture as Texture option determines which additional options are available.

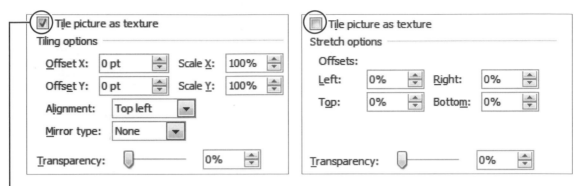

When Tile Picture as Texture is selected, a certain set of options appear.

Tile Picture as Texture

When the Tile Picture as Texture checkbox is selected, the image used for the background (texture, picture file, or clip art) repeats across the entire slide.

The image file (above) repeats across the slide (right).

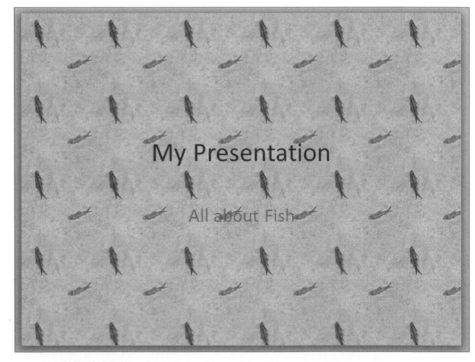

When the Tile Picture as Text option is selected, the available options include Offset, Scale, Alignment, and Mirror Type. Changing the Offset X option shifts the tiled background to the right (if a positive value is entered) or left (if a negative value is entered). The Offset Y option shifts the background up or down. The Scale X and Scale Y options resize the image being used as a tile (you cannot resize greater than 100%). The Alignment option can be used to further reposition the background on the slide, and is best used by experimentation. Last, the Mirror Type option flips the image horizontally or vertically as it's being tiled. This option also is best used by experimentation.

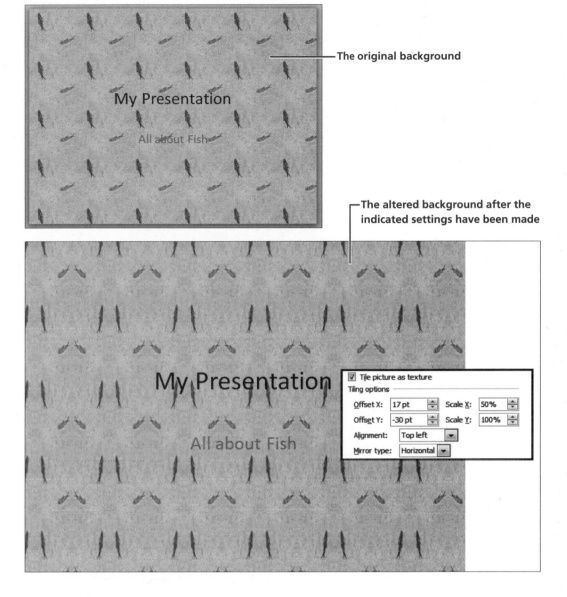

The original background

The altered background after the indicated settings have been made

Do Not Tile Picture as Texture

When the Tile Picture as Texture option is not selected, the image used for the background (texture, picture file, or clip art) resizes to fill the slide without repeating. If the picture is small, this can result in a blurry image, as in the following figure.

The image file (above) enlarged to fill the slide (right)

When the Tile Picture as Text option is not selected, the available options include a series of stretch offsets for left, top, right, and bottom. As these values are increased or decreased, the image stretches. For example, altering the Left offset works from the left side of the image. An offset of 0% results in the image being placed directly up against the left border. Positive values push the image into the slide, while negative values pull the image away from the slide. Similarly, increasing the Bottom offset squishes the image toward the top, while decreasing the Bottom offset stretches the image down toward the bottom.

Imagine you were standing in the computer screen next to the slide. A positive value in any of these offsets would instruct you to push the image away from you, toward the inside of the slide. A negative value would instruct you to pull the image toward you, out of the slide.

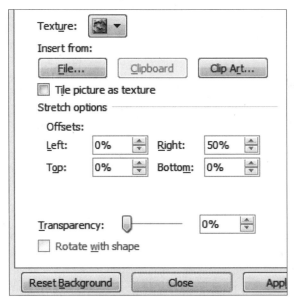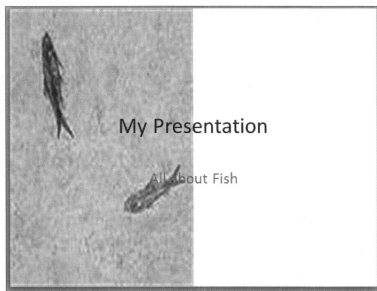

A Right offset of 50% pushes the picture from the right, half way across the slide.

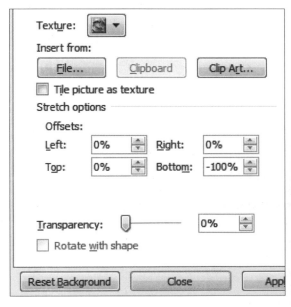

A Bottom offset of –100% pulls the picture down from the bottom.

Task	Procedure
Use a texture as a slide background	■ Choose Design→Background→Background Styles→Format Background from the Ribbon. ■ Choose the Picture or Texture Fill option. ■ Choose a texture from the Texture menu. ■ Click Close to apply the gradient to the selected slide(s). *or* ■ Click Apply to All to apply the gradient to all slides.
Use clip art as a slide background	■ Choose Design→Background→Background Styles→Format Background from the Ribbon. ■ Choose the Picture or Texture Fill option. ■ Click the Clip Art button to display the Select Picture dialog box. ■ Select the clip art image you want to use and click OK. ■ Increase or decrease the Offset values to stretch the picture to fit the slide. ■ Click Close to apply the gradient to the selected slide(s). *or* ■ Click Apply to All to apply the gradient to all slides.
Use an image file as a slide background	■ Choose Design→Background→Background Styles→Format Background from the Ribbon. ■ Choose the Picture or Texture Fill option. ■ Click the File button to display the Insert Picture dialog box. ■ Browse to the image file you want to use and click Insert. ■ Increase or decrease the Offset values to stretch the picture to fit the slide. Negative values stretch or compress the picture off of the slide. Positive values stretch or compress the picture in toward the slide. ■ Click Close to apply the gradient to the selected slide(s). *or* ■ Click Apply to All to apply the gradient to all slides.

Apply Texture and Picture Backgrounds

In this exercise, you will apply a texture background and a clip art background.

Apply a Clip Art Background

1. If necessary, select the second slide, **Our Services**.

2. Choose **Design→Background→Background Styles→Format Background** from the Ribbon and follow these steps to open the Select Picture dialog box:

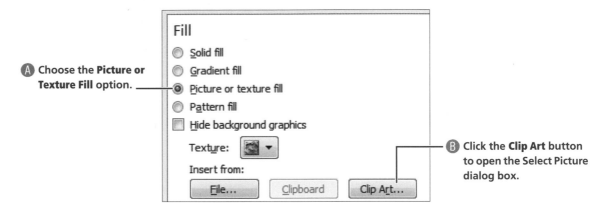

3. Follow these steps to apply a clip art background:

The clip art image is added as a slide background, but the Format Background dialog box remains open so you can change the settings.

4. Follow these steps to modify the background image:

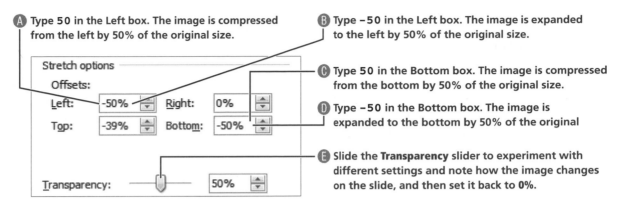

Ⓐ Type **50** in the Left box. The image is compressed from the left by 50% of the original size.

Ⓑ Type **-50** in the Left box. The image is expanded to the left by 50% of the original size.

Ⓒ Type **50** in the Bottom box. The image is compressed from the bottom by 50% of the original size.

Ⓓ Type **-50** in the Bottom box. The image is expanded to the bottom by 50% of the original

Ⓔ Slide the **Transparency** slider to experiment with different settings and note how the image changes on the slide, and then set it back to **0%**.

A background image is too busy for this presentation. You will replace the clip art background with a textured background.

Apply a Textured Background

5. Follow these steps to apply a texture background:

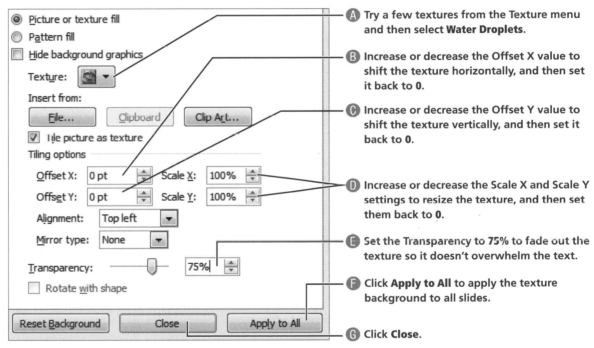

Ⓐ Try a few textures from the Texture menu and then select **Water Droplets**.

Ⓑ Increase or decrease the Offset X value to shift the texture horizontally, and then set it back to **0**.

Ⓒ Increase or decrease the Offset Y value to shift the texture vertically, and then set it back to **0**.

Ⓓ Increase or decrease the Scale X and Scale Y settings to resize the texture, and then set them back to **0**.

Ⓔ Set the Transparency to **75%** to fade out the texture so it doesn't overwhelm the text.

Ⓕ Click **Apply to All** to apply the texture background to all slides.

Ⓖ Click **Close**.

6. **Save** 🖫 your presentation.

Saving a Customized Document Theme

Video Lesson   labyrinthelab.com/videos

After you have modified the color scheme, fonts, and/or background styles of a presentation, you may want to save your modified theme as a custom theme. The custom theme will be available to apply to new presentations just as with any built-in document theme. Your custom theme will even be available to other Microsoft Office applications. Your PowerPoint presentations can match your word processing documents created in Microsoft Word when your custom theme is applied to both.

Theme Location

Custom themes are saved to your computer in a folder associated with your Windows user name. Any custom themes saved in this location will be available directly from the Design→Themes command group from the Ribbon. You can also browse for and apply a custom theme stored somewhere else on your computer; however, such a theme won't be directly accessible from the Ribbon.

Customized document themes are saved by default in the C:\Documents and Settings\ <username>\Application Data\Microsoft\Templates\Document Themes folder on Windows XP and in the C:\users\<username>\AppData\Roaming\Microsoft\Templates\Document Themes folder on Windows Vista and Windows 7. Any custom themes saved in this location will be available directly from the Design→Themes command group from the Ribbon.

 Many computer labs prevent saving a custom theme to the default location. However, you can always save your custom theme to your USB Flash drive or other location. Applying the custom theme would then require a few more steps because it would not be available from the Ribbon.

Deleting a Custom Theme

If your custom theme was saved to the default location, you can remove it from the Ribbon by deleting the theme file from the Document Themes folder. You can do this manually by navigating to the folder and deleting the file, or automatically from the Ribbon. Deleting the custom theme file will not affect any presentations that currently use the theme; you just won't be able to apply the custom theme to future presentations. Similarly, if you move a presentation with a custom theme to another computer that does not have the custom theme in the default location, your presentation will still use the custom theme.

Task	Procedure
Save a custom theme to the default folder	■ Choose Design→Themes→More ⊽ →Save Current Theme. ■ Type a name for your theme and click Save. ■ Your custom theme is saved to the default location and is available directly from the Design tab on the Ribbon.
Save a custom theme to a different location	■ Choose Design→Themes→More ⊽ →Save Current Theme. ■ Browse to an alternate location, such as your USB Flash drive. ■ Type a name for your theme and click Save. ■ Your custom theme is saved to the alternate location and is not directly available from the Ribbon.
Apply a custom theme	■ If the custom theme was saved to the default location, choose Design→Themes and select your custom theme. ■ If the custom theme was saved to an alternate location, choose Design→Themes→More ⊽ →Browse for Themes. ■ Navigate to the location where you saved your custom theme. ■ Select the custom theme and click Apply.
Delete a custom theme	■ If saved to the default location, choose Design→Themes→More ⊽ from the Ribbon. ■ Right-click your custom theme and choose Delete from the pop-up menu.

DEVELOP YOUR SKILLS 8.1.5

Save and Use a Custom Design Template

In this exercise, you will save your custom document theme and apply it from the Ribbon.

Before You Begin: Check with your instructor to see whether you are able to save a custom theme to the default location or whether there is another specific location in which to save your custom theme.

Save the Custom Theme

1. Choose **Design→Themes→More** ⊽ →**Save Current Theme** from the Ribbon.

2. In the File Name box, type **Green Clean Water**.

3. If you have permission to save in the default location, click **Save** and skip to **step 5**. Otherwise, continue with **step 4**.

4. Use the **Save Current Theme** dialog box to browse to the location suggested by your instructor and then click **Save**.

Apply a Custom Theme

5. Choose **File→New** to open the New Presentation dialog box.

6. **Double-click** the Blank Presentation icon to create a new presentation.

7. Type **Green Clean** for the slide title.

8. Type **Custom Theme** as the subtitle.

9. Choose **Design→Themes→More** ⊽ from the Ribbon.

10. If your custom theme was saved to the default location, continue with **step 11**. If your custom theme was saved to an alternate location, skip to **step 15**.

Default Location

11. Select your custom **Green Clean Water** theme from the Custom row of the All Themes menu.

12. **Save** your presentation as `Green Clean Custom Theme`.

13. Choose **File→Close** to close the presentation and return to the previous presentation.

14. **Skip** the rest of this exercise and continue with the next topic.

Alternate Location

15. Click the **Browse for Themes** option at the bottom of the Themes menu.

16. Navigate to the location where you saved your custom theme.

17. Select your custom theme file and click **Apply**.

18. **Save** your presentation as `Green Clean Custom Theme`.

19. Choose **File→Close** to close the presentation and return to the previous presentation.

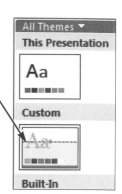

8.2 Using Slide Masters

Video Lesson   labyrinthelab.com/videos

PowerPoint slide layouts and designs are based on master slides. The masters store all of the design elements, including the font styles and sizes, placeholder sizes, background design, and color schemes. Any changes made to a slide master are inherited by all the slides based on the master. This is a great way to easily insert a company logo or other design element on every slide in a presentation. For example, adding a logo to the slide master causes every slide based on that master to also display the logo.

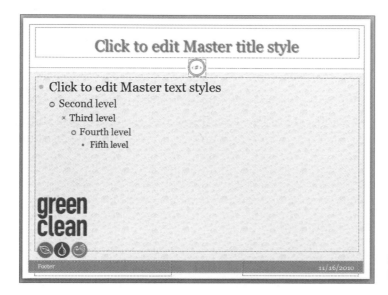

Slide master with a logo inserted in the bottom-left corner.

All slides based on the slide master inherit the changes to the slide master, such as the logo being inserted.

Using Slide Masters and Layout Masters

PowerPoint's document themes each have 12 master slides. There is one slide master and 11 layout masters. Both types of masters play specific roles.

- **Slide master:** The slide master is the basis from which all layout masters take their initial characteristics. Anything on the slide master is inherited by each of the 11 layout masters. However, layout masters can be further customized to be unique from each other (and from the slide master itself).

- **Layout masters:** It is the layout masters that define what the various slide layouts look like, such as the Title Slide, Title and Content, or Two Content layouts.

Changes to master slides affect the current presentation only and do not permanently alter the document theme.

Slide Master View

You can view the slide masters in Master view, which is similar to Normal view with a scrollable slides panel on the left side of the screen. Pointing to any of the slide thumbnails displays a pop-up ToolTip with information about how many slides in the current presentation use that particular master.

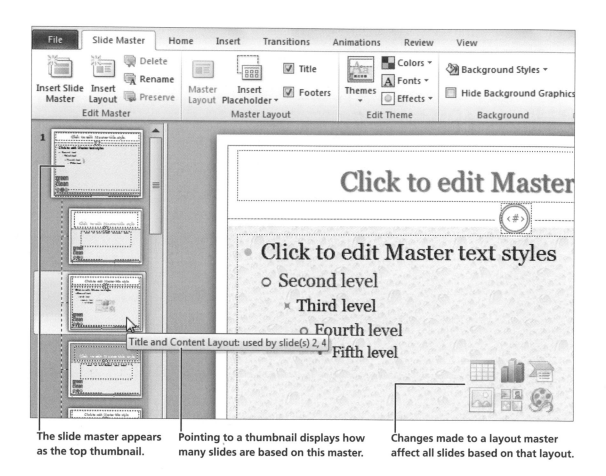

The slide master appears as the top thumbnail.

Pointing to a thumbnail displays how many slides are based on this master.

Changes made to a layout master affect all slides based on that layout.

QUICK REFERENCE | **EDITING MASTER SLIDES**

Task	Procedure
Edit a master slide	■ Choose View→Presentation Views→Slide Master from the Ribbon to enter Master view.
	■ Select a slide master from the left side of the screen.
	■ Make any changes you like to the slide master.
	■ Choose Slide Master→Close→Close Master View from the Ribbon to exit Master view.

DEVELOP YOUR SKILLS 8.2.1
Edit Slide Masters

In this exercise, you will edit slide masters to see the effect on presentation slides.

Change Text Formatting

You will change all the slide titles for current and future slides to display a text shadow.

1. Choose **View→Master Views→Slide Master** from the Ribbon to enter Master view.

2. Follow these steps to select a slide master:

Ⓐ Point to the **first slide master** on the left of the screen and notice the ToolTip indicating that this master is used by slides 1–4.

Ⓑ Click the first slide, **Green Clean Water Master.**

3. **Drag** to select the title text *Click to edit Master title style.*

4. Choose **Home→Font→Text Shadow** from the Ribbon.

5. Choose **Slide Master→Close→Close Master View** from the Ribbon to exit Master view.

6. Select each slide in Normal view and note that the slide titles all display a text shadow.

Add a Visual Element

7. Choose **View→Master Views→Slide Master** from the Ribbon to enter Master view.

8. Select the first slide master, **Green Clean Water Slide Master**.

9. Choose **Insert→Images→Picture** from the Ribbon.

10. Browse to the Lesson 08 folder, select the **PNG image file** Green Clean logo, and click **Insert**.

11. Drag the image to the **bottom-left corner** of the master slide as in the following figure.

12. **Click** a few other slide masters on the left of your screen and notice that they all display the Green Clean logo image.
Changes made to the first slide master affect all other slide masters and all slides in the presentation.

13. Choose **Slide Master→Close→Close Master View** from the Ribbon to exit Master view.

14. Select each slide in Normal view and note that the Green Clean logo image appears on every slide.

15. Select the second slide, **Our Services**.

16. Try to move the Green Clean logo image.
You can't. The image exists on a master slide, so it can be moved or deleted only from the master slide.

17. **Save** 🖫 your presentation and continue with the next topic.

8.3 Using Action Buttons

Video Lesson   labyrinthelab.com/videos

Action buttons allow you to add buttons to your presentations that can provide for slide navigation, opening of files, or other tasks. Action buttons contain widely recognized symbols for navigation and information commands, such as Next, Previous, Information, Document, and Sound. Action buttons are especially useful for creating a presentation that will be controlled by others, such as a presentation running on a sales table at a conference.

Action buttons for navigating a slide show at the bottom of a slide

Identifying Action Buttons

All action buttons, except custom buttons, have built-in functions that run whenever that button is clicked in Slide Show view. ToolTips make it easy to identify the function of an action button when you choose it from the menu.

A ToolTip displays when you point to an action button on the Ribbon.

To quickly add action buttons to all slides in your presentation, place them on a master slide.

QUICK REFERENCE	USING ACTION BUTTONS
Task	**Procedure**
Insert an action button	■ Choose Insert→Illustrations→Shapes ▼ from the Ribbon.
	■ Point to an Action button along the bottom row of the menu to see a ToolTip that identifies the action button.
	■ Click the action button to load your cursor.
	■ Drag on the slide to draw the action button. The action button appears on your slide already formatted for the document theme.
	■ In the Action Settings dialog box, click OK to accept the default action associated with the button, or select a different action and click OK.
Change the action of an action button	■ Select the action button.
	■ Choose Insert→Links→Action from the Ribbon to display the Action Settings dialog box.
	■ Choose a new action and click OK.

Formatting Action Buttons

Action buttons do not have a preset size. After selecting an action button from the Ribbon, your cursor changes to a crosshair icon that you can use to draw a boundary for the action button. You can drag a small area to create a small button, or a large area to create a large button. Sometimes you will have several action buttons on a slide, and they will not all be drawn at the same size. PowerPoint has a variety of commands available from the Ribbon to size all the action buttons the same and to align them to each other.

Action buttons may initially be drawn at different sizes anywhere on the slide (left). Use Ribbon commands to make all the buttons the same size, aligned, and evenly distributed (right).

QUICK REFERENCE	FORMATTING ACTION BUTTONS
Task	**Procedure**
Make all action buttons the same size	■ Select one action button on the slide. ■ Press Shift, click the remaining action buttons, and then release Shift. ■ Choose the Drawing Tools→Format tab from the Ribbon. ■ Locate the Size command group and type a value in the Shape Height and Shape Width boxes to make the buttons the same size.
Align action buttons to each other	■ Select one action button on the slide. ■ Press Shift, click the remaining action buttons, and then release Shift. ■ Choose the Drawing Tools→Format→Arrange→Align ▼ menu from the Ribbon. ■ Select one of the top six Align options in the menu to align the buttons to each other.
Evenly space action buttons	■ Select one action button on the slide. ■ Press Shift, click the remaining action buttons, and then release Shift. ■ Choose the Drawing Tools→Format→Arrange→Align ▼ menu from the Ribbon. ■ Select Distribute Horizontally or Distribute Vertically to evenly space the action buttons.

DEVELOP YOUR SKILLS 8.3.1
Create Action Buttons

In this exercise, you will insert action buttons on a master slide to control movement forward and backward in your presentation.

Insert Action Buttons on a Master Slide

1. If necessary, select the second slide, **Our Services**.

2. Choose **View→Master Views→Slide Master** from the Ribbon.
   Remember, anything you place on a slide master appears on all of the slides based on that master.

3. Point to the third slide master, **Title and Content Layout**.
The ToolTip indicates that this master is being used by slides 2 and 4.

4. Choose the **Insert→Illustrations→Shapes ▾ menu** from the Ribbon.
PowerPoint displays a menu of available shapes. The action buttons are at the very bottom of the menu.

5. Follow these steps to place the Back, Home, and Next action buttons on slides 2–5:

Ⓐ Click the **Back** action button. (Your insertion point changes to crosshairs.)

Action Buttons

Ⓑ Point to an empty area of the slide master, drag **down** and to the **right** to draw a small rectangle, and then **release** the mouse button.

PowerPoint displays a dialog box with the preset action for this button. In this case, there's no need to modify the action.

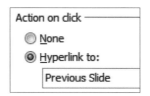

Action on click
◯ None
◉ Hyperlink to:
　Previous Slide

6. Click **OK** to accept the default button action.

7. Repeat **steps 5 and 6** to add a Next action button and a Home action button, as shown at right.
Don't worry if the action buttons aren't the same size or aligned—you will fix that in the next few steps. Your slide should resemble the following figure.

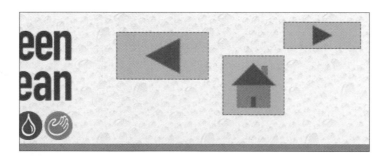

8. Select one of the action buttons, **press** Shift, **click** once on each of the remaining action buttons, and then **release** Shift.
All three action buttons are selected (display handles).

9. Follow these steps to size the action buttons:

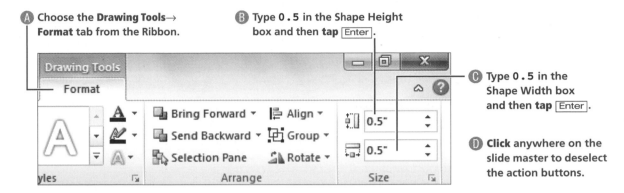

Ⓐ Choose the **Drawing Tools→Format** tab from the Ribbon.

Ⓑ Type **0.5** in the Shape Height box and then **tap** ⌷Enter⌷.

Ⓒ Type **0.5** in the Shape Width box and then **tap** ⌷Enter⌷.

Ⓓ **Click** anywhere on the slide master to deselect the action buttons.

10. Drag the **Next** button to the lower-right corner of the slide master, as in the following figure.

11. Drag the **Home** and **Back** buttons next to the Next button, as in the following figure. (Don't worry about aligning the buttons perfectly. You will use a Ribbon command to align the buttons.)

12. Using the ⌷Shift⌷ key, select all three buttons.

13. Choose **Drawing Tools→Format→Arrange→Align→Align Top** from the Ribbon.
The buttons shift to become top-aligned.

14. Make sure all three buttons are still selected and, if necessary, **drag** them back down toward the bottom corner of the slide master, as in the following figure.
Now that the buttons are in the desired general location, you will use a Ribbon command to distribute them evenly.

15. If necessary, use ⌷Shift⌷ to select all three buttons.

16. Choose **Drawing Tools→Format→Arrange→Align→Distribute Horizontally** from the Ribbon.
PowerPoint spaces the buttons evenly.

17. Choose **Slide Master→Close→Close Master View** from the Ribbon.

18. Display the **title slide**.

    Notice that there are no action buttons on this slide. (Remember that you added the action buttons only to the Title and Content layout master, not to the Title layout master.) There is no slide before the title slide, so no Back button is needed. The title slide is the home slide, so no Home button is needed. Although clicking anywhere on a slide advances to the next slide, users may not know they need to click to start the slide show. Therefore, you will place a Next action button on the title slide.

19. Display slide 3, **Products Sold**.

    The Products Sold slide does not include the action buttons because this slide does not use the Title and Content layout master. You will copy the action buttons to the Two Content Layout master.

Copy and Paste an Action Button

20. Choose **View→Presentation Views→Slide Master** from the Ribbon.

21. Select the third slide master, **Title and Content Layout**.

22. Select all three **action buttons** and choose **Home→Clipboard→Copy** from the Ribbon.

23. Choose the **Two Content Layout** master from the thumbnails at the left of the screen and then choose **Home→Paste**.

    The action buttons are pasted and will now be included on any slide that uses the Two Content layout. You will now copy and paste the Next button to the title slide.

24. Select the **Next** button only and choose **Home→Clipboard→Copy** from the Ribbon.

25. Choose **Slide Master→Close→Close Master View** from the Ribbon.

26. If necessary, select the **title slide**, and then choose **Home→Clipboard→Paste** from the Ribbon.

    The Next button is pasted in the same location on the title slide.

Test the Buttons

27. Choose **Slide Show→Start Slide Show→From Beginning** from the Ribbon.

28. Click the **Next** action button (or anywhere on the title slide) to advance to the next slide.

29. Use the **action buttons** to navigate forward, back, and home.

30. **Tap** $\boxed{\text{Esc}}$ to end the slide show.

31. **Save** the presentation.

Cleaning Up

| Video Lesson | labyrinthelab.com/videos |

If you have created and saved a custom document theme to the default location, it is available directly from the Ribbon. If you have created and saved a custom color scheme, it is automatically available directly from the Ribbon. If you are using a shared computer such as one in a classroom or school computer lab, you should delete these customizations so other people can use PowerPoint in its default state.

Delete Customizations

In this exercise, you will delete custom color schemes and custom document themes that are directly available from the Ribbon.

Remove Custom Color Schemes

1. Choose the **Design→Themes→ Colors** menu and locate any custom color schemes listed at the top of the menu.

2. **Right-click** the custom color scheme and then choose **Delete** from the pop-up menu.

3. Choose **Yes** when prompted to delete the theme colors.
   The custom color scheme is deleted and is no longer available from the Ribbon.

4. Repeat **steps 1–3** for any additional custom color schemes.

Remove Custom Document Themes

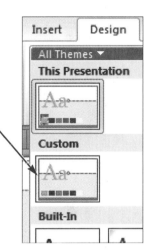

5. Choose **Design→Themes→More** ⎐ from the Ribbon to display the Themes menu.

6. Locate any custom themes listed at the top of the menu.

7. **Right-click** the custom document theme and choose **Delete** from the pop-up menu.

8. Choose **Yes** when prompted to delete the theme.

9. Repeat **steps 5–8** for any additional custom themes.

10. **Exit** PowerPoint.

8.4 Concepts Review

Concepts Review   labyrinthelab.com/pp10

To check your knowledge of the key concepts introduced in this lesson, complete the Concepts Review quiz by going to the URL listed above. If your classroom is using Labyrinth eLab, you may complete the Concepts Review quiz from within your eLab course.

Reinforce Your Skills

Customize a Color Scheme

In this exercise, you will customize the color scheme of the rs-Tropical Getaways Custom presentation.

Use a Built-in Color Scheme

1. **Start** PowerPoint and **maximize** the program window.

2. **Open** the rs-Tropical Getaways Custom presentation from the Lesson 08 folder.
   The current color scheme uses mainly blue. The word Tropical *suggests that more green should be used.*

3. Choose **Design→Themes→Colors→Metro** from the Ribbon.
   The colors on every slide change to that of the Metro theme. However, the green is a bit too bright.

Create a Custom Color Scheme

4. Choose **Design→Themes→Colors→Create New Theme Colors** from the Ribbon.

5. Look closely at the Theme Color labels and match the colors in the dialog box to the actual colors on the slide. The main colors currently in use are as follows:

Label	Where Used
Text/Background – Dark 1	Bulleted text color on slides 2–4
Text/Background – Light 1	Slide background
Text/Background – Dark 2	Slide titles
Accent 1	Large green block at the bottom

6. Change the colors as follows (remember to point to each color in the menu and pause to see a ToolTip with the color name):

Label	Color to Use
Text/Background – Dark 1	Light Blue, Text 2, Darker 75% (from the fourth column)
Text/Background – Light 1	Light Blue, Text 2 (from the fourth column)
Text/Background – Dark 2	Green, Accent 1, Darker 50% (from the fifth column)
Accent 1	Green, Accent 1, Darker 25% (from the fifth column)

7. Type **TG Custom** in the Name box and then click **Save**.
   The custom color scheme is automatically applied to all slides and is available directly from the Ribbon.

8. **Save** your presentation.

Customize a Slide Background

In this exercise, you will customize the slide backgrounds.

Before You Begin: You must have completed Reinforce Your Skills 8.1, and the rs-Tropical Getaways Custom presentation should be open.

Apply a Built-in Theme Background

1. Choose the **Design→Background→Background Styles** menu from the Ribbon and point to a few of the backgrounds tailored for the document theme.

2. Select the **Style 9** background in the lower-left corner of the menu.
   The background adds some texture (diagonal lines) and is automatically applied to all slides. Perhaps a more exciting background would be a better choice.

Apply a Solid Background Color

3. Choose **Design→Background→Background Styles→ Format Background** from the Ribbon.

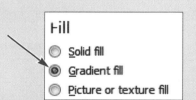

4. Choose the **Solid Fill** option.

5. Choose a **light green** color from the Color menu.

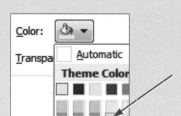

The color is applied to the current slide. Perhaps a gradient background would give the slide more depth.

Apply a Gradient Background Color

6. Choose the **Gradient Fill** option.
   PowerPoint automatically creates a gradient based on the current background color. Feel free to experiment with the gradient settings.

Apply a Tiled Background Picture

Solid and gradient colors just don't scream excitement like an actual background photo will for this particular presentation.

7. Follow these steps to insert a clip art picture as a slide background:

Ⓐ Choose the **Picture or Texture Fill** option.

Ⓑ Click the **Clip Art** button. Wait while the Select Picture dialog box loads the thumbnails.

Ⓒ Type **palm tree** and then click **Go**.

Ⓓ Select an appropriate photo and then click **OK**.

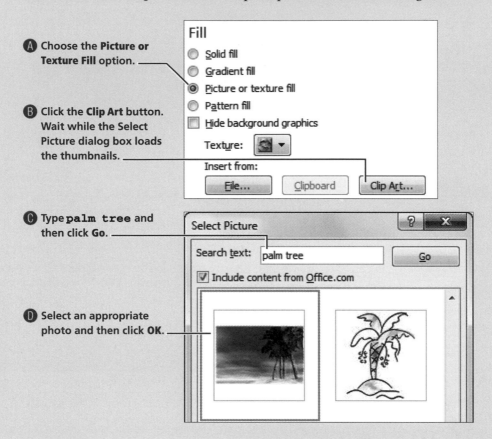

The photo is applied to the current slide, but is much too dark and obscures the text.

8. Set the Transparency to **80%**, click **Apply to All**, and then click **Close**.

The background is applied to all slides.

9. Save your presentation.

Work with Master Slides

In this exercise, you will edit master slides.

Before You Begin: You must have completed Reinforce Your Skills 8.2, and the rs-Tropical Getaways Custom presentation should be open.

Add a Company Logo

1. Choose **View**→**Master Views**→**Slide Master** from the Ribbon.

2. Select the third slide master, **Title and Content Layout**, which is used by all but the title slide.

3. Choose **Insert**→**Images**→**Picture** from the Ribbon.

4. Navigate to the Lesson 08 folder, select the **TG Logo** image file, and click **Insert**.

5. Drag the image to the **lower-right corner** of the slide, but not to the actual edges of the slide. *You won't be displaying slide footers, so the overlap of the image on the footer is okay.*

6. Choose **Slide Master**→**Close**→**Close Master View** from the Ribbon to return to Normal view. *The logo appears in the bottom-right corner of all slides except the title slide.*

Add Action Buttons

7. Choose **View**→**Master Views**→**Slide Master** from the Ribbon.

8. Select the first slide master, **Concourse Slide Master**, which is used by all slides.

9. Choose **Insert**→**Illustrations**→**Shapes**→**Action Buttons**→**Back**.

10. **Drag** anywhere on the slide to draw the action button.

11. When the Action Settings dialog box appears, click **OK** to accept the default action of navigating to the previous slide.

12. Repeat **steps 9–11** to add Home and Next action buttons. Your slide should resemble the following figure.

13. Using the ⌈Shift⌉ key, select all three buttons.

14. Locate the **Drawing Tools**→**Format**→**Size** command group in the Ribbon.

15. Set both the Shape Height and Shape Width to **0.5**.

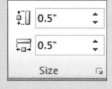

16. Drag each of the buttons to the **top-right corner** of the slide and loosely arrange them as in the following figure.

17. Use the [Shift] key to select all three buttons.

18. Choose **Drawing Tools→Format→Arrange→Align→Align Top** from the Ribbon to align the buttons.

19. Choose **Drawing Tools→Format→Arrange→Align→Distribute Horizontally** from the Ribbon to evenly space the buttons horizontally.

20. Choose **Slide Master→Close→Close Master View** from the Ribbon to return to Normal view.
    The buttons appear in the top-right corner of all slides.

21. Choose **Slide Show→Start Slide Show→From Beginning** and use the action buttons to navigate the slide show.

22. **Tap** [Esc] when you reach the Contact Us slide to end the slide show and **save** your presentation.

Save and Delete a Customized Document Theme

In this exercise, you will save your customized Tropical Getaways Custom theme.

Before You Begin: You must have completed Reinforce Your Skills 8.3, and the rs-Tropical Getaways Custom presentation should be open.

Save a Custom Theme

1. Choose **Design→Themes→More** ⊽ **→Save Current Theme** from the Ribbon.

2. Type **Tropical Getaways** in the File Name box.

3. If you are allowed, **save** the theme to the default location. Otherwise, browse to your USB Flash drive or other storage location and **save** the theme.

4. If you saved to the default location, choose **Design→Themes→More** ⊽ from the Ribbon and notice that your custom theme is available directly from the Ribbon.

Delete a Custom Theme and Color Scheme

5. If you saved your theme to the default location, choose **Design→Themes→More** ⊽ from the Ribbon.

6. **Right-click** your custom Tropical Getaways theme and choose **Delete** from the pop-up menu.

7. Choose **Yes** when asked to delete the theme.

8. Choose the **Design→Themes→Colors** menu from the Ribbon and locate the **TG Custom** color scheme you created earlier in Reinforce Your Skills 8.1.

9. **Right-click** the TG Custom color scheme and choose **Delete** from the pop-up menu.

10. Choose **Yes** when asked to delete the theme colors.
    Both the custom theme and custom color scheme have been deleted, but your presentation has not been affected. You will not be able to apply the theme or color scheme to future presentations.

11. **Exit** PowerPoint.

Apply Your Skills

Edit Slide Masters and Add Action Buttons

In this exercise, you will add action buttons to a slide master.

1. **Start** PowerPoint and **maximize** the program window.

2. **Open** the as-Classic Cars Custom presentation from the Lesson 08 folder.

3. Display the Slide Master view and add **Back**, **Home**, and **Next** action buttons so they appear on every slide.

4. Use your best judgment as to the placement of the buttons, but make sure they are all the same size and appropriately aligned. Your slides may resemble the following figure.

5. **Run** the slide show to test your action buttons, and then return to **Normal** view.

6. **Save** your presentation.

Customize a Document Theme

In this exercise, you will customize the color scheme and background.

Before You Begin: You must have completed Apply Your Skills 8.1, and the as-Classic Cars Custom presentation should be open.

Customize and Save a Document Theme

1. Experiment with different **built-in color schemes** until you find one that you like.

2. Edit several colors (such as title, text, or background colors) to create a **custom color scheme** named `CC Custom`.

3. Customize the background by using a **gradient fill** or a **texture** of your choice.

4. **Save** the customized theme as `Classic Cars Theme`. Note whether you are saving to the default location or to an alternate location.

5. **Save** and **close** your presentation.

Apply a Custom Theme

6. Choose **Office**→**New** from the Ribbon, and then **double-click** Blank Presentation to begin a new presentation.

7. **Create** a presentation on a topic of your choice. Be sure to include at least four slides.

8. Apply the custom **Classic Cars Theme** you created in the first part of this exercise. *Remember, if you saved your theme to an alternate location and your custom theme is not available from the Ribbon, you will have to use Design→Themes→More ▼→Browse for Themes to locate and apply your theme.*

9. **Save** your presentation to the Lesson 08 folder as `as-[Your Name] Custom`. (Substitute your actual name for *Your Name*.)

APPLY YOUR SKILLS 8.3

Remove Customizations

In this exercise, you will delete your custom settings from the Ribbon.

1. **Delete** the CC Custom color scheme from the Ribbon.

2. If you saved your Classic Cars Theme from Apply Your Skills 8.2 to the default location, **delete** it so it no longer appears on the Ribbon.

3. **Exit** PowerPoint.

Critical Thinking & Work-Readiness Skills

In the course of working through the following Microsoft Office-based Critical Thinking exercises, you will also be utilizing various work-readiness skills, some of which are listed next to each exercise. Go to labyrinthelab.com/workreadiness to learn more about the work-readiness skills.

8.1 Customize and Save a Document Theme

The Green Clean marketing department is trying to unify all advertising materials so they share a common look and feel. Create a new presentation of at least four slides, apply a design theme that supports the Green Clean marketing message, and add slide titles and placeholder text to indicate this is a presentation to be used as a starter for future presentations. Create a custom color scheme to change the theme colors. Change the slide backgrounds. Save both the presentation (as **ct-Green Clean Starter**) and the custom theme (as **ct-Green Clean Theme**) to your Lesson 08 folder. Delete the custom color scheme from the Ribbon so it does not interfere with other students' work.

WORK-READINESS SKILLS APPLIED

- Organizing resources
- Seeing things in the mind's eye
- Thinking creatively

8.2 Edit Slide Masters and Add Action Buttons

Start with the ct-Green Clean Starter presentation you created in the previous exercise and save a copy of it as **ct-Green Clean Custom** to your Lesson 08 folder. Add the Green Clean logo (Lesson 08 folder) to one of the slide masters so it appears on all slides. Add action buttons to aid navigation. Feel free to add any other action buttons you think might be useful. Format the action buttons so they are equally sized and spaced. Save your changes.

WORK-READINESS SKILLS APPLIED

- Organizing and maintaining information
- Seeing things in the mind's eye
- Thinking creatively

8.3 Use a Custom Theme

Copy the custom theme you created in the first Critical Thinking exercise for this lesson to your USB drive, if necessary. Swap USB drives with another student and copy their custom theme to your Desktop. Return the borrowed USB drive and make sure to get yours back. Open the ct-Green Clean Custom presentation you created in the previous exercise and save it to your Lesson 08 folder as **ct-Green Clean Alternate**. Apply your partner's custom theme to your presentation. Make any necessary creative changes to the slide master or fonts to improve the design theme. Save the changes to your presentation.

WORK-READINESS SKILLS APPLIED

- Participating as a member of a team
- Thinking creatively
- Seeing things in the mind's eye

Index

Notes

Notes

Notes

Notes

Notes